When Between Pillars - *Push!*

By

Meka Anniece Parrish

This book is a work of non-fiction. Names and places have been changed to protect the privacy of all individuals. The events and situations are true.

© 2003 by Meka Anniece Parrish. All rights reserved.

No part of this book may be reproduced, stored in a retrieval system, or transmitted by any means, electronic, mechanical, photocopying, recording, or otherwise, without written permission from the author.

ISBN: 1-4140-1712-X (e-book)
ISBN: 1-4140-1713-8 (Paperback)

Library of Congress Control Number: 2003098192

This book is printed on acid free paper.

Printed in the United States of America
Bloomington, IN

1stBooks — rev. 12/02/03

TABLE OF CONTENTS

Chapter One	Made In His Image	1
Chapter Two	Consider My Servant	17
Chapter Three	Failing And Falling	35
Chapter Four	Lukewarm	47
Chapter Five	Demons? In The *Church?*	75
Chapter Six	Still Not Ready	85
Chapter Seven	Notice For Testing	99
Chapter Eight	The Test	113
Chapter Nine	Push!	125
Chapter Ten	God Is My Light	137
Chapter Eleven	Happy In Jesus Christ	149

Thank you, Jesus Christ, for forever changing my life! Special thanks to my mother, Denice "Queen" Parrish, for always being "there" for me and to my dad, Charles "Mike" Parrish, for encouraging me to publish my testimony. Thank you, Pastor V.C. Scott, for allowing me to have a chance to showcase every gift that God gave me! Last, but not least, thank you, Sister Daphne Coles, for being trustworthy and for all your pre-editorial assistance!

I LOVE YOU ALL!

CHAPTER ONE

Made In His image

One of the happiest and most joyous days in a woman's life is the day she gives birth to her first child. The anticipation that builds for months and months as she picks out baby clothes complementary to the expected baby's sex and imagines a child she has never seen before wearing them and playing with other children, smiling and doing everyday things is beyond words. Who knows how many false labors she's had prior to the day of birth, as she excitedly awaits her baby? The baby she feels moving in her belly every day. The baby she can already see in her mind's eye as she watches her expanding belly lovingly in the mirror as she gets dressed in the bathroom. There is something special about being able to have your own baby; adoption is great also, but there is no feeling like carrying a life inside you. A baby. A blessing.

> *Before I formed thee in the belly I knew thee; and before thou*
> *Camest forth out of the womb I sanctified thee, and ordained thee*
> *A prophet unto the nations.*
>
> Jeremiah 1:5

When I was born I was diagnosed a hemispheric child. That meant everything on my left side, from the neck down to my feet, was considerably larger than everything on my right side. I had severe varicose veins in my legs and vital organs. Being hemispheric, the veins on the larger side would pump blood well and it would flow normally and sometimes very quickly through my body, but when the blood from the left side got to the right side there would be too much blood coming too fast because the right side was so much smaller than the left. When that happened there would form a blockage. The blood would pile up in the smaller veins and sometimes clot, or worse, the veins would pop without warning causing me to have to undergo several emergency surgeries. My feet were webbed, like ducks' feet, and my ankles were like swollen wrists. The doctors told my mother I would not live to see my first birthday; the disease would surely kill me; but if by some miracle I survived to see my first birthday, I would be confined to a wheelchair because of the severity of the deformities in my feet and legs. The bad news got worse: should I be "lucky" enough to live to adulthood I would never conceive because of the differences and misplacement of my vital organs.

This was my mother's first child; can you imagine how she felt? No mother likes to think something is wrong with her baby, or to be told the baby will die. Having a child puts you in such an emotional whirlwind: one minute you are happy and the next overwhelmed, and here it is hours after my birth and they tell this poor woman the child she has carried, nourished and protected; the child that grew in her body, the child she is already attached to will die in a year's time. I wonder what she thought?

When Between Pillars - Push!

> *I will praise thee; for I am fearfully and wonderfully made...*
>
> Psalms 139:14

Living past my first birthday was not very easy for me. While other babies were drooling and learning the skills fundamental for motor coordination, countless emergency visits and operations made me an almost permanent resident in the nearby hospital. By the time I was ten months old I was having epileptic seizures on a regular basis. These seizures were hard to identify because I didn't tremble or shake as in the convulsive seizures we know about today; I would just stare into space. My brain was seizing and my body was not. The seizures were often triggered by tile floors that were common in the bathrooms of homes in the late 1970s and early 1980s. I was being potty trained, and I would sit on my potty chair and stare at the floor and go into a seizure. Usually, when I came out of the seizure I would be screaming or crying. I was afraid to go into the bathroom for months because of this.

The doctors used words like thrombosis (meaning a blood clot in the heart or blood vessels) and hemotoma (when the blood does not clot correctly) and endometrioses (extreme pain) to explain to my mother what was going on in my body. When they got one problem under control, another would arise out of nowhere.

What made it worse was that they could not understand why being hemispheric would cause so many problems. Having one limb larger than the other should not cause seizures and ruptured veins. It should not cause swollen lymph nodes on the face and under the arms. It should not cause moles on a child's body to mutate and take on cancerous looks. It should not cause a person to experience rectal prolapse because the walls are so weak they collapse when trying to pass a stool. They really did not know how to treat it, because being hemispheric should have been as simple as the name, but for some reason it was not. Nobody knew any preventative measures to take to keep me out of surgery.

As I reached preschool age I was able to walk like the other kids, much to the amazement of the doctors, but my feet were the size of those of a child in first grade, and the kids in my class noticed something was different about my legs. Nothing on me looked like anything on them. What is really funny to me now, is that *I* thought I looked like everyone else. I never noticed I had a problem until other kids started asking questions. Soon the question, *What happened to your feet?* sounded like an insult. I was made fun of so much by my peers that I fought anyone who mentioned my feet or my legs. It did not matter if they really wanted to know or if they were truly concerned about me.

People did not know how to react to my deformities. It would not have been so bad if just the kids acted up, but their parents were talking about me also. One day when my family and I went out to eat, I was walking alone to the buffet to fix a plate for myself. My mother, who was a single parent, was letting me exercise my newfound independence. I happened to be wearing shorts that day and I could feel the stares of people looking at my legs as I tentatively fixed myself a plate. As I walked away from the buffet I overheard one lady telling her mother that the veins in my legs were AIDS. Her children were with her and she made a big deal of keeping them away from me. I didn't even know what AIDS was! It had not yet been a big deal in the '80s like it is now. But I could tell by the tone in her voice that it was not a compliment. I never told my mother about this incident. I always felt I had to be a big girl for her. She had enough to think about.

By the time I got to the first grade I was back in the hospital and had been hospitalized for what seemed like months. I had been there so long I was in the hospital schooling program. Most of my friends were cancer patients, since at that time they were the only people who actually lived in the hospital. We were all confined to wheelchairs, no matter who thought they were well enough to walk, and we'd wheel ourselves to the room that served as the lesson room. When we were finished, we would race our wheelchairs down the ramps of the hospital hallways back to our rooms.

I suppose the doctors put me in that wing of the hospital because they did not know anything about what it was to be hemispheric. There were few known cases then. So they treated me like I had cancer also. When they would bring a cup of pills to the girl with whom I shared a room, they would bring one for me also. I was confined to a wheelchair and strung to an I.V. just like the children with cancer. I slept in a metal crib, and every few hours someone was poking, x-raying and running tests on me. They were amazed I had lived so long with so many problems and also wanted to learn more about my condition.

I became famous with the staff very quickly. Doctors would come in with Polaroid cameras to take pictures of my legs and feet. They said it was to help them treat other patients. Then they asked to take pictures for an encyclopedia and a science book. (For years I wondered if I would open a book in science class and see myself.) I had become a human lab rat to the hospital. They tried drug after drug on me, shot after shot. They wanted all the documentation they could get, all in the name of helping some unknown soul who may have the same condition as me. I felt like: if I'm the only person in the world with this thing, let me take it to my grave!

That same year scoliosis started to develop in my spine. Being hemispheric had made the left side so big and it had grown so much faster than the right side that one of my hips was actually lower than the other, causing my back to curve. I remember one day after they had x-rayed the curve in my back the doctors said they wanted to put a brace on it to correct it. At that time I was so tired of sleeping in metal cribs, blood samples, shots, x-rays, not to mention the countless photos, all I could imagine was that metal crib swallowing my back in brace form. I yelled, "Whatever it is, let it kill me!" and I stormed out of the x-ray room with tears in my eyes. I was a six-year-old first grader and I wanted to die.

> *Rejoice, and be exceeding glad: for great is your reward in heaven:*
> *For so persecuted they the prophets which were before you.*
> Matthew 5:12

Before every operation my mother and I had what became a ritual. She had been doing it since before I could remember. She would ask me right after I was prepped for surgery, "Who loves you?" and I'd say, "Jesus." She would always smile at me as I was wheeled away. At this time in my life I had so many questions for God. None of them were "Why me?" They were much too sophisticated for a six-year-old to be thinking. I wanted to know what the big idea was. God made handicapped people, deaf, mute, blind and people we consider normal. All these people belonged to a group and I wanted to know where my group was. I was not blind, deaf or mute. I was too normal to be handicapped, and too handicapped to be normal.

Where did I fit? Besides, I thought, if Jesus loved me so much he should let me die so I could be with him. He should not let the doctors butcher me and take pictures of me.

When I would sit at church under my grandmother, the preacher would say, "God don't give you no mo' than you can bear." But I felt like he had already given me too much. I was so young!

The day my mother withdrew me from the hospital against the doctors' will, they threatened her saying if she withdrew me from the hospital I would die. She felt that if I stayed, they would kill me. In her mind I had a better chance at home with my praying grandmother and my grandfather who was a minister. She had given me to God at birth, so as far as she was concerned He would have to fix me. We pulled the I.V.'s out of my arms because the doctors would not. She dressed me and we left. I never wanted to see another hospital again as long as I lived.

I went to summer school so that I could keep up with my class and that year I attended second grade like a normal kid. I had friends who always wanted to play with me at recess and always wanted to sit with me at lunch. They always wanted to be next to me at show and tell and I always had neat toys to talk about then. I loved reading and music. When it was time to say the Pledge of Allegiance and sing "My Country 'Tis of Thee", I was the loudest singer in the class. Other kids wanted me to teach them to sing like I did. Some of my classmates would call me at night and we would practice the song together so we would be ready for the next day. I sat near a cute boy in class. He did not know I had a crush on him. (Especially since back then, girls still had cooties.) I loved my teacher. I made straight A's. Everything was great!

I often wondered why none of the kids in my family thought I was built funny. I was in the children's choir at church and I would sing to the glory of God as loud as my little lungs would let me, and no one in the children's choir thought I was handicapped or built funny, neither did the children in my class at school, unlike at the other school. No one thought anything was wrong with me, yet every doctor in the state wanted me for research. On top of that, I was alive and having a great time. For the first time in my young life I enjoyed living and I actually wanted to live.

When Between Pillars - Push!

One day, towards the end of recess, I was playing with a few of my classmates by the stairs leading to our classroom. We could not wait to get inside and do the little cut and paste projects that second graders do. We wanted to be the first ones in the line when it was time for us to line up.

I suppose others started to notice the time also, because there was a nice line forming behind us and the teacher had come out of our classroom to stand at the top of the stairs to make sure no pushing or hair-pulling went on as we were lining up. It was as I stood in line that I felt something wet in my panties. I thought, *"Oh great. I just peed in my pants."* This would normally embarrass a child, but in our class it was an everyday thing. It was almost a fad, because everyone was doing it. There was one boy in my class who peed his pants everyday. He did it so much that the teacher moved his desk to the back of the class so if he wet himself, he would be the only kid wet.

I, however, just kept wetting on this occasion, until not only my panties were wet, my pants were getting damp also. I felt the front of them to see just how wet they really were. I wondered if I could still wear them home, but when I brought my hand up it was bloody! My heart raced, I quickly surveyed the other children in line to see if anyone had noticed my pants. No one had noticed because they were too busy talking to each other and playing in the line. Trying not to bring too much attention to myself, I whispered my teacher's name in a stage whisper and kind of waved my hand. When she did not notice, I decided to go to her before anyone noticed what had happened.

"I'm wet," I told her. She looked at me confused. I was not one of the wetting children. Before she could ask any questions, I rambled on. "I need to go to the nurse's office." My eyes were tearing up now. Everyone knew that when you were wet you went to the office to get extra pants and not to the nurse. She realized there was a problem and had the other kids stay out for recess longer.

"God, please let this be simple, please don't let me go to the hospital. In Jesus' name, Amen," I prayed, as honest as I knew how and with everything I had. On the way to the nurse's office I explained to my teacher that I was bleeding and she went to call my mother while the nurse gave me new panties, a pair of pants and something that looked like a pillow. She showed me how to put it in

my panties, and after I was changed my teacher and I entered an empty classroom to talk.

She asked me if this was the first time I had had a period. *PERIOD?* I had no idea what that was. I assumed it was what you call bloody pants. I nodded that it was, as I concentrated on balancing my little behind on that pillow the nurse put in my panties. It felt like I was on sitting on a seesaw! I thought I would fall off. I certainly felt taller sitting on it.

My teacher was still talking about the changes in a woman's body when my mother came. I started to think that there was nothing wrong at all, that I had only caught my period. I was more convinced when my mother and my teacher went to the corner to whisper about this period thing.

Wait till I tell the girls I got my period, I thought with a sigh of relief. Everything would be ok. I would not have to go back to the hospital and I could go on with my life.

But it was not my period, and before I knew it we were back in the hospital and I was sitting in a metal crib waiting for an I.V. to be put into my already scarred arms.

I had been there so many times, my arms looked like I had the chicken pox.

This time they had to do emergency surgery. One of my veins had burst and for some odd reason my blood would not clot. I had already lost enough blood to make me dizzy and I was starting to get nervous. I sang in my head so that no one could hear but God and me, just to calm my nerves. *Do Lord, Oh Do Lord, Oh Do you remember me?* I sang the words in my mind. I was going to bleed to death if they did not fix it right then. *Do Lord, Oh Do Lord, Oh Do you remember me?* Two doctors came with the I.V. machine. They did not wait until I was ready for them to stick me. They just put the rubber band on my arm and stuck the needle in. My heart felt like it was dying as the liquid filled my veins. *Do Lord, Oh Do Lord, Oh Do you remember me?* My mother interrupted my thoughts. "Who loves you?" she asked breathlessly. My eyes filled with angered tears. "Jesus," I mumbled through gritted teeth. She smiled and they wheeled me away in my metal jail cell of a crib. *Way beyond the blue...*

I was determined to die this time. I was going to be with Jesus. I was sick of being stuck and poked and stared at. I was sick of the gray bars on my bed. I was sick of the hospital smell. I was sick of bald kids everywhere! I was sick of masked men behind cameras. I was sick of life. What was Jesus doing to me? I thought he loved me!

CHAPTER TWO

Consider My Servant

Until that moment I thought this test was my mother's test. How strong she had to be to watch me go through so much pain and adversity and not say anything but that Jesus loves me. Was she wondering if Jesus loved her? I would have asked God that: if he loved me so much why did this happen to my child? And, if that's love, who needs hate?

I realize now this was my test. Not because I had done something so horrible that I had to be punished. God knew what he created and how he created it. He knew my purpose. He knew what the end would be. He knew I would be a strong witness for Him in the end, even if the beginning looked a little rocky. So he said, *"Have you considered my servant, Meka?"*

I hadn't even been born on earth when he asked, but I existed before the foundations of the earth. I worshipped before I got to earth and God was bragging on this: *"there is none like her in the earth...one that feareth God, and escheweth evil"* (Job 1:8). Then Satan answered the Lord and said, *"doth Meka fear God for naught?"* In other words, does she fear you for nothing? You're going to let me touch her? The apple of your eye?

Now Satan was apprehensive…Satan knows every blessing the Lord has given you. He keeps track of them. He can run off your blessings to others, if he wishes to make them jealous. Isn't it odd how your enemies know about everything you own? They know where you live, what kind of car you drive, who you're married to and how many kids you have. They know everything about you except your social security number; and for a small fee they can get that on the Internet and find out more.

Satan says in Job 1:10, "*Hast not thou made a hedge about him* [add your own name here]*, and about his house, and about all that he hath on every side? Thou hath blessed the work of his hands, and his substance is increased in the land.*" Now, *how* does Satan know all of this unless he is meddling in your business? He is all up on God's business and what God is going to do. He cannot even do his *own* job correctly for running behind what God has already done, being nosey, gossiping. The adversary can tell God what blessings we have received from God in detail, and it scares him.

Some people know so much of your business and they spend so much time running behind you wanting to destroy what you're doing, that they end up destroying themselves. They know how blessed you are but they still want to come against you.

Satan was asking all these questions because he wanted to be sure he would not be trapped by God (or set up for the WOO-WOO, as kids say). Satan knows the scripture that says, "*Touch not* my anointed." Some of us are God's anointed. Now here it seems like God is saying, "*Touch*". Something isn't right and Satan wants to know what it is. He knows God is not a man that he should lie, nor the son of man that he should change his mind. What's going on here?

He's afraid of God and what will happen if he does something to us. If you look at the next verse he tries to hype up his own head. He has got to get himself excited to do this thing. He feels he's being challenged. Here's a chance to get back at God for kicking him out of heaven. Here, he's got to make his powers seem like more than they really are. He cannot shut God's Kingdom down, yet he says in Job 1:11, *"put forth thine hand now, and touch all that he* [you can put your name here] *hath, and he will curse thee to thy face."* In other words, "Are you sure you want to let me loose on them, God? Do you know who I am? Do you know what I can do? Don't you know I kill, steal and destroy for the fun of it?"

But be not deceived, God is not mocked. Satan and his threats do not faze God. I can imagine God shrugging his shoulders in a nonchalant way and saying, "Do *you* know who *I* am? *I AM* the I AM. I AM the beginning *and* I AM the end. I AM the first *and* I AM the last. I AM the Alpha and Omega. *I saw* you fall from heaven like lightning before the earth was created. You think you got game?"

Then the Lord said unto Satan, *"Behold, all that he hath is in thy power: Only upon himself put not forth thine hand..."*

See, Satan still cannot touch without permission from God. But he will do, and has done, everything he can to make you and Job *think* you have been touched. Remember when you were younger and would have a disagreement with a brother, sister or a cousin or friend. When you were angry, you would say, "Don't touch me!" And he or she would then put a hand or a finger in your face as close as he or she could without touching and sing, "I'm not touching you, I'm not touching you, I'm not touching you!"? Even when we stepped back or moved to the right or left, that person's hand would still be so close you could smell it and he'd still be singing, "I'm not touching you." Now, you could turn around and do the same thing back to him, but then there would just be two people with their hands in each other's faces, screaming, "I'm not touching you!" The only way to make that person move his hand was to call on your parents or hit the person hard enough to make him stop.

In my case it seemed like everything I had was in Satan's power but he could not touch me. I was too little in the Word of God to hit him back. I only knew so much Word, and I had no idea what a prayer warrior was back then. All I could do was to call on Jesus. Satan could try to speak death on me through the medical staff over and over until I believed it or until he broke my spirit and my will to live. He could take pictures of me until I felt less than human. He could cage me in a metal cage with other souls while he was in the process of trying to destroy my self-esteem. He could have my peers say that I wasn't normal so I would be angry enough to live in sin, knowing the Bible said be not angry and sin not. That way he'd have a doorway to touch me.

But he did not expect my focus to stay on Jesus. And he forgot Psalms 51:17, which says, *"The sacrifices of God, are a broken spirit: A broken and a contrite heart, O God, Thou wilt not despise."*

When that vessel broke in my body I was a young lamb in Christ. Satan thought he had won, but because there is life in the blood, it became like the sacrificial blood at Passover. It was the blood of a lamb spread on the doorpost so the death angel had to pass over the Israelites. It was the blood from a lamb in Christ spread on me when the vessel popped so the death angel had to pass over me. What Satan meant for bad, God made good. In John 4:10 it says, "Jesus answered and said unto her, *if thou knewest the gift of God, and who it is that saith to thee, Give me to drink: thou wouldest have asked of him, and he would have given thee living water.*" What is even better is that while I was singing to the Lord, asking if he remembered me, he was already hooking up the I.V. and telling me he did. And when the doctor put the I.V in my arm, out came the living water I had asked about. Jesus had already been there, working where I couldn't see.

> *This is he that came by water and blood, even Jesus Christ;*
> *Not by water only, but by water and blood...*
>   I John 5:6

The only reason I felt I was dying inside was because my flesh was being slayed. I did not want to miss what the other normal kids were doing at school. I did not want to have another operation. I wanted just to walk out of the hospital and be healed. Sometimes God works like that, and sometimes he does not. But he does work nonetheless.

When Between Pillars - Push!

After that particular operation, I did not wake up immediately. I was in a coma for a whole week and did not know it. The doctors had operated on me three times during my coma and finally just threw up their hands to my mother saying they did not know what else to do. They did not know how to bring me out. They did not know how to deal with my situation. They could not fix me, but they finally found out what my disease was called. It was Klipple Trunany Webber, and there have been only eight people on this entire planet known to have it to the extent I was afflicted.

When I woke up I was like a heathen child. *Where was Jesus?* I pulled the oxygen mask off and violently thrashed about the bed. Doctors ran to restrain me for fear of me popping my stitches. I screamed when my eyes focused on the metal bars of my bed. *Why wasn't I in heaven?* I pulled the I.V. clear out of my arm and started to yank at the other wires that were hooked to machines. My little arms flailed about so fast that the only limbs the doctors could restrain were my legs. Other medical personnel rushed to assist. Everyone was in panic and the room was in chaos. "I WANT MY MOM!" I screamed, thrashing in that violent rage. *Nothing I ever want to happen happens.* Two doctors rushed out of the double doors to get my mother. I had begun to cry and scream. I almost growled in anger. In seconds my mother was by my side, whispering. She whispered so softly I had to stop screaming and moving to hear her.

I could smell her perfume and her hands were cool to my flesh as she stroked my hair. "Shhh...Jesus loves me, this I know, for the Bible tells me so. Little ones to him belong; they are weak but he is strong." By the time she got to the chorus of "Yes, Jesus loves me," I was totally sedated. My mother had a way of coaxing you to sing when you did not want to. She could not sing well at all...but she kept singing until I started to mumble the words, too.

Sometimes God is trying to bring us out of a situation scott-free and we're so caught up in the fact that something did not go the way we thought it should have gone that we forget to look at what he has already brought us out of. Sometimes we are so busy throwing hissy-fits, kicking and screaming and undoing everything God has set up for us to receive the blessing; and complaining "Why God?" that it becomes difficult to hear him.

A long time ago someone said to me, "Sometimes God whispers." And I huffed and said, "Well that's too bad, because I usually scream." Sometimes if two people are screaming, no one is listening. Both are talking over each other and arguing. God will not argue. He speaks and he whispers but he will not let us bring him to our level. If he did, he would not be God; He would be us.

We are like children. When you see a child yelling or upset and crying and you whisper at that child, even in her ear, she has *got* to be quiet to hear what you say. There are times she will still try to yell while you are whispering in her ear, but she cannot listen to you and concentrate on yelling at the same time. She has to choose one or the other, and most times the whispering party wins.

Every once in a while you will get a totally rebellious child who has to be dealt with in a more *loving* manner (if you get my drift). The "laying of hands" on a child is not always as we envision. It may truly be corporal and physical. And may not be to increase her faith but to teach her wisdom.

In my case, this type of "laying of hands" would not have been appropriate. But God knows what tactic to use with each one of his children. He knows our thoughts afar off and he always reminds us that he cares for us. In my case it was through song, in your case it could have been a card or flowers someone sent with a word of inspiration, a phone call when you needed it or something as simple as a hug. Remember the Lord that keeps us neither slumbers nor sleeps. He's the beginning and the end. He's the only God that can drop you off, carry you through, and be there when you get there all at the same time. He is always a lifetime ahead of us.

Be still and know that I am God...
Psalms 46:10

Once I was still I could hear the song my mother was singing and I began to sing with her. I started to regain sight. Even though I was going through all of this turmoil, Jesus still loved me. And just because I did not go to heaven when I wanted to go, it did not mean I would not go. I had to wait until I did what God put me on earth to do. I could not just go because I was fed up with someone poking me and taking pictures and caging me up. I was created to bless his holy name. I was supposed to glorify God in all things. I was to trust in the Lord with all my heart and lean not unto my own understanding. I was to acknowledge him even in sickness and pain.

What if Jesus had been like us when it was time to give his life for our sins? It was obvious he did not want to die the kind of cruel death he would have to face. He asked repeatedly for the cup to be passed. If you read Luke 22:44, it talks about him being in agony and praying until great drops of sweat dripped like blood from his head. How many of us pray like that when we do not want to do something God has already said has to be done? He prayed hard for this thing not to go down like it did, but in the end he said, *"not my will but thy will be done."* This is *not* what we usually do. Sometimes we pray hard and cry and moan and then we get up and say, "All right, Lord, you know if it were anything else, I would do it. But I can't do *that* for you."

What if Jesus had decided he was not going to hang on that cross for all of us on earth to have a right to the tree of life? What if, when the Pharisees and the authorities showed up to arrest him in the garden of Gethsemane, he had bolted through the crowd and escaped? What if he had killed everyone there, just because he did not want to do the will of God? Even worse, what if he had taken his own life because the authorities were after him and he was not going to "go out like that"? What then? You see how important it is to do the will of God? It is true that none of us are dying to redeem the world, but he has a purpose for all of us and it is not to "play God."

It is funny that as long as we are dancing, shouting, financially secure and got everything "goin' on," we call ourselves blessed and highly favored. But there were countless people in the Bible who were blessed and highly favored who did not always have everything they wanted. Joseph was blessed and highly favored, but his own family sold him into slavery. Daniel was blessed and highly favored and he was thrown into a lions' den. Let us not forget David, who slew Goliath with a rock and a slingshot! If that is not highly favored, I do not know what is! But he, later, had to watch his back because King Saul was always out to kill him. Uriah was blessed and he basically died because someone (David, again) wanted to get with his wife. Moses was highly favored from the basket ride to Pharaoh's daughter, and even after he killed an Egyptian. But he did not follow directions well and it cost him the Promised Land. Jesus' earthly

When Between Pillars - Push!

parents were highly favored but they could not even get a room to give birth to Jesus in that night because there were none left. Various apostles were blessed and highly favored but Stephen was stoned to death; Paul was thrown in prison, beaten with rods three times and stoned; they all were running for their lives just for associating with Jesus. Jesus' cousin, John, was highly favored. He baptized Jesus, but he was decapitated.

What I am trying to get you to understand is that just because hard times fall on you, it does not mean you have lost the favor of God. It does not mean you are not blessed. In fact, be concerned if everything is going smoothly all the time because then you may not be as much of a threat to the kingdom of Satan as you think you are. All these people did not stop doing the will of God when hard times fell upon them; they kept pressing toward the high mark of the calling. Satan attacks those who are not his already. That does not mean we as Christians should not prosper. It does mean new level new devil.

In my Church we sing a song called "Sacrifice of Praise". The words are:

> We bring the sacrifice of praise
>
> Into the house of the Lord!
>
> We bring the sacrifice of praise
>
> Into the house of the Lord!
>
> And we offer up to you,
>
> The sacrifices of thanksgiving
>
> And we offer up to you
>
> The sacrifices of joy!

I don't know who wrote it, but, this song has special meaning to me because it is easy to praise the Lord when all your bills are paid and you got a little money in the bank, your kids are doing well in school, your marriage is going great, the job wants to promote you and you are not sick or hurt. So when the choir sings your favorite song and the minister preaches on the topic you like, you say, "Yeah, girl, we had some Good word!" Oh, it is easy to praise then.

But what about when your bills are due and you just got the electric notice, your child is failing some classes, and your baby's daddy or mama has not even *thought* about paying child support for the last six months? Your job is relocating and they are not taking you with them. You have the 'flu or some other debilitating sickness. You go to church and it seems like every song the choir sings is dead, and the preacher gets up and preaches on fornication, drugs and "playing church" and you know you and your live-in are living together and are not married (but you are playing house) and every night you fire up a joint with some friends and drink a little brew and the music you are bumpin' to is not Kirk Franklin, Hezekiah Walker, Fred Hammon or CeCe Winnans?

It is at this time praise needs to become sacrifice. It is not easy to do, but you do it because you are thankful to the Lord for all he has done. You are giving your praise as a sacrifice and giving it gladly, because it is all you have to give. You are joyful about where God has brought you because you may not be where you want to be, but you are not where you used to be.

There are always worse problems to have than the ones we have. I would complain to my grandmother that my feet were too big and my legs were ugly. She would just look at me and say, "Well, what if you didn't have no feet? Be thankful you got the ones you got, because you could have been born without any at all!" Then she'd ramble on about a man with no legs. Now what could I say to that except to thank God I have feet and legs? Hallelujah for working feet and legs.

But it is hard to see all that goodness when you are in the midst of a situation. And it is hard to fight the urge to want to "help God" do it. We pray to the Lord, *"Lord help me pay my bills, help me be anointed, help me to hold out, help, help, help,"* and then when nothing happens in our time, we say, *"Well, I'm just going to keep my tithes and offerings to myself so that I can pay my bills."* Or *"Sister so and so has the gift of prophecy so I'm going to learn it from her!"* Prophecy may not be the gift God has for you. He may want you to be an evangelist or maybe the head usher where the anointing flows on you daily. Yet, we brush it off like, *well God knows my heart.* Yes he does know it; *do you?* Do you realize that the motives behind rushing the plan of God are usually, *selfishness, greed, and jealousy?* We want to look good in the eyes of someone else. Be careful saying that God knows your heart. You need to know your heart. The only time we say, *"well, God knows my heart,"* is when we are about to do something we *know* we should not do!

It may seem as though I am coming down very hard on you, but that is only because I have been down the path most traveled and I do not want you to do the same thing. If you are already down that path, I want you to know what hell awaits, so that you will turn around now.

When I finally got out of the hospital and got off the medicines and got away, I was like a caged animal set free. I did not say it out loud, but on that trip home I vowed to myself, *I will never ever, as long as I live, step foot in a hospital again.* Not for a vaccine, a check-up or anything. I did not care how much pain my syndrome put me in. I was going to make up for lost time and have fun with some kids who were not sick. The only way I was going back to the hospital was in a body bag! I swore on it.

CHAPTER THREE

Failing and Falling

As the years went by, I almost got my wish. I ran with the wrong crowd, got involved in gang activity, started selling drugs and smoking them. At first, it started as a black and mild (a smoke) on the roof of my house when my mother was gone. I then began smoking weed, a joint here and there while I was bagging up dimes and twenties to sell. Eventually, I was smoking blunts and going to school a little high. I hung with the guys because I was a tomboy. No one at school knew this innocent face that sang in the choir at church, was involved in school musicals, sang in the show choir, won singing awards in LA, and was voted best voice in her high school class, was involved in the stuff I was involved in.

I tucked my flag in my pocket when I went to school and I guess people thought it was just a hair rag. I was involved in so many school activities that my hair was always messy. (That and the fact I called it "expressing myself" when my hair was all over the map.) I didn't think I was cute at all. A lot of people called me bigfoot and sasquatch. With my big feet and varicose veins in my legs, the hump on my back had expanded to the point that one of my classmates touched it with concern, saying, "Ooooh, Meka, are you all right?" I shrugged it off.

I looked to the guys as my refuge. There could be one of the ugliest guys in the world at your school and if you went up to the best looking guy in the class and said something negative about the ugly guy, the cute guy would say, "Hold up, dat's my dog." With girls, it was all designer. You had to have your hair done and lipstick and the short skirt showing off the pretty legs…Ugh! I hated girls.

I was this type of girl: a guy I thought was real cute would come up to me and lean against the wall next to me, lick his lips slowly and say, "Hay Meka...what's up with your girl? Hook me up." It happened so many times I just started acting like one of the guys. Hanging out on the wall with my pants baggie and a huge shirt that was, like, ten sizes too big. Wearing black men's boots and gymshoes and sometimes braiding my hair back like the guys did. Or some days just twigging it up. I would drag race in my Jimmy truck against guys in my class at like ninety miles per hour on the expressway. (Incidentally some people I knew died like that.)

I hated myself. I was drinking and causing trouble in my classes with my teachers, some more than others. I had a very short temper and was always getting in altercations. I wasn't a big girl, but I lifted weights like a maniac, just in case. A lot of people envied me. I didn't know why, but a lot of girls wanted to be able to sing like me, and have my eyes, and grow hair as fast as I could and just be like me. Many girls younger than I looked up to me and I threw them away like people did to me without even realizing.

I had a very close friend, and we are still close today. She would say to me, "You would be real pretty if you wore some clothes that fit, girl. With that small waist and your height, and those eyes…that face…" I just blocked her out. I looked at her like she was the bombshell. To me, beautiful was little feet, pretty legs, that curve in a woman's back that guys go crazy about. That is one thing for sure I didn't have because of the wretched hump that scoliosis had put on my back! It didn't matter if a girl's face was not all that cute. All the guys cared about was the body anyway.

I didn't have a real boyfriend until I was in the tenth grade. Everyone else had play dates way before I did. I will never forget this one guy. I had stopped praying for so many years I had almost forgotten how. Besides, it seemed to me that every time I prayed, it did not work. I always prayed that my back, my feet, and my legs would be healed.

But when God did not move like I expected, I started praying just that my back would be healed. I could live with everything else. I thought maybe I had asked for too much. I tried everything, including the Psychic Network (which was happy to see me coming because I talked to them for $1.99 a minute like they lived next door!). I wrote my prayer request on a piece of paper and anointed it with oil. I even tried the name-it and claim-it stuff that was really hot with the churches in the 1990s. Nothing worked.

I, then, totally stopped praying. Why? I thought God did not hear me. One day I cried and cried that I wanted to be pretty like the other girls and have a boyfriend, too. It seems silly now, but it was a real big deal then. I prayed for years for this guy I had seen in church!

Let me stop here. A lot of times we spend our time praying for things not meant for us. If we do it long enough, we seem to make God weary. We use his name on any little thing. "In the name of Jesus, give me a car", "In the name of Jesus, give me a man/woman", "In the name of Jesus, give me the winning lotto number so that I never have to work again." Not "Jesus, I need a car to take your people to church," or "Jesus, I'm satisfied with you being my comforter, thank you for blessing me." And, how dare we play the lotto and pray for God's blessing when we're not supposed to be playing the lotto anyway? God does not bless over any mess!

Well, I was full of mess and had the audacity to ask for what I thought would be a blessing. But after a couple of years, God let me date the guy I asked for who attended my church. He was almost four years older than me and I think he drove a beat-up old Chevy. The thing was dangerous! The passenger seat was held up by a baseball bat, the ceiling was collapsing, the seats were torn, the car actually growled, it had no steering fluid and when you pressed the brake to stop, it seemed to say, "Who me? Oh!" The car exploded in my driveway several times. We dated for about three years. I was proud of my man and his car! I asked him to pick me up all the time. He was more embarrassed about the car than I was. We were in bliss for about a year. Then it got rocky.

He wanted to have sex with me and I was scared. God would not like that. God did not like me drinking, smoking and cursing either but *this* seemed like a bigger sin than all of those put together. Now I know there is no such thing as a big sin and a small sin. God hates all sin!

I had also heard that you would bleed the first time you had sex. All I could think of was the operation I had had in the second grade. I told him, "Let's wait till we are married." And he tried for about six more months and then he dumped me for someone who would do what I wouldn't do. I was devastated!

I called him and asked when he would be my boyfriend again, but he said he needed to sow his wild oats. *Was this the guy I prayed for?* I could not speak. I felt numb and I also felt like I could not get anyone else because I was so ugly. I felt that I *had* to keep this guy. It seemed as though there would not be anyone else. What really bothered me was that he had the audacity to still want to be friends.

For the next six months I did more gang activity than I had ever done. It was an outlet for me. I started hanging out in the city late at night and I was selling drugs to crack heads. I did almost anything, just to get my mind off this guy. Anything but pray. God had failed me again! I never thought once that I had failed God.

I got in more trouble with the police in those six months than I care to recall. Countless warnings and a few overnight trips to the station. It was hideous and it was all because my focus was on some man and not God. I do not know if God got tired of me messing up my life or what, but finally the guy came back to me. Like an idiot, I took him back. But it was never the same. I always ended up worrying if he was cheating. Plus, he had a "thing" for white girls that I felt was really ridiculous. I love my white sisters, but I'm not one. So it made my complex worsen: the man I loved, loved a woman I wasn't. Every time we would go out he would make comments about various girls' bodies. I was so stupid to stay in that relationship. But I did not know any better. I thought I had to keep this guy for the rest of my life or I might never have a chance at marriage, or anything else, to be happy.

On top of that I slept with him. If that was not a night for the devil, I don't know what was! The bleeding myth was true. I bled so much I thought I would have to get another operation. I lost so much blood that by the time he brought me home I was lightheaded, running a fever and in a cold sweat. I slept in the car as I thought, *I'm going to die right in this car.* But I didn't die. I just felt like it.

Have you ever been in a situation where you thought you were going to die and you knew you weren't living right? When I was out in the world there were many times I thought I would die. **Don't act like I'm the only one.** Some of us who smoked weed got "laced" by someone we thought was a friend, and instead of dying the Lord let us hyperventilate, or vomit or just let them pump our stomachs at the hospital. He let us think we were going to die. Or the first time we had some real liquor, trying to hang with the guys and went on a vomit binge, we woke up with a headache so bad it hurt to think. We then prayed to God for death, yet we lived. Then there were those of us who were involved in illegal activities and everyone got shot or caught by the police and only we remained to tell the story. Or some of us were out there sleeping around and we knew we were married and the girl we cheated with thought she was pregnant, or she had a boyfriend back in 1981 who just died from AIDS and maybe she passed it to us. We then find out she's negative and so are we! HAY! That's shouting stuff to be delivered from. And what did we always say? "Thank you, *Jesus*. I'll *never* do that again!" That is a witness of how he protected us when we did not deserve it. That is a witness of his grace and mercy.

But some of us are hard headed and we do not hear the gentle whispers of God. Some of us think we did it on our own and by our own might we survived, just because we were "cool like that." Then we end up right back in the situation we were delivered from. If there is anyone who needs to be saying, "Why?" it is God. Why, after he continually blesses us, are we not satisfied? Why do we always blame God when things go wrong?

If we had just kept on the straight and narrow, none of this would have happened in the first place! But Noooooo! "Thanks God, I got it from here." That is what we always say. That is what I always said. And I went with the devil because it looked like I was missing something. The devil is not our friend! The only thing I was missing was God.

The thing that made it even more ignorant of me was that I believed what the devil told me. He said I was ugly, I was going to die, nobody loved me or would love me. "Every time someone looks at you the first thing they notice is your deformities," the devil said, and I believed him and put myself with his people. The first thing a person would do was look me up and down and scope me out for something wrong. The devil had me praying for death so that he could say, "See, I told you," to the Lord, but I never cursed God, and that was what he was trying to get me to do. But I couldn't.

*Train up a child in the way he should go: and when he is old,
He won't depart from it.*
                                                     Proverbs 22:6

What Satan had forgotten was there was something placed in me from the womb to be on Christ's side. God gives every man a measure of faith. My mother took that measure and stretched it until she could not stretch it anymore. She nurtured that seed in me at a young age. She always pointed me to Jesus in the midst of all my struggles with life. With every surgery I had, I grew stronger in the Lord. True, I did not want to get strong the way I did, but according to Romans 5:3-5, *"tribulation worketh patience; and patience, experience; and experience hope and hope maketh not ashamed; because the love of God is shed abroad in our hearts by the Holy Ghost which is given to us."*

When I was a sinner, Christ died for me, for you, and anyone else who accepts him. I do not care about who knows what I used to do. I am not that person anymore. I am a daughter of God. If God is for me, who can be against me?

If I had known then what I know now, I would never been involved in those gang/occult meetings, or carried a Black & Decker staple gun in my jeans (just in case somebody got wild.)I would have never watched the people I associated with levitate over ouiga boards and learned all those chants. I never did feel comfortable when they got into all that demonic stuff. Someone always asked me to float. I was always saying, "If God wanted me to fly, I would have had wings." What a great testimony in the midst of lighting a blunt and cracking open a brew!

I was so confused as to what I wanted to do. Did I want to be saved? Did I want to be lost? One minute I was preaching and the next minute I was cursing. What had my life become?

I had been working a regular job in the day and living for the devil at night. I had more money than I knew what to do with from selling crack and weed. (Incidentally, I have none of it now.) Yet I was drinking every night to get away from myself. The more I drank to get away, the more I kept hearing my own thoughts. I could not get away from me, and I was very depressed and unhappy. I needed direction, so I decided to go to church.

CHAPTER FOUR

Lukewarm

People tend to forget that there are real hurting people in church who need help and it has taken all the strength they could muster up to walk through the door. Some people put their masks on before they enter the church and then take them off when church is over, and some people carry their masks in their hands, up to the altar, and lay them down. The Word of God says in Matthew 11:28, *"to come unto me all ye that are weary and heavy laden and I will give you rest."* But sometimes when a drug addict, a dope pusher, a prostitute, or an unwed mother comes into the church, or just anyone with a problem that has been riding them so hard you can see the results on their faces, church folk tend to shun them. We may say, "How dare he come to church with crack pipe burns on his lips!", or "Oh no! She ain't sitting next to me smelling like last night!" We then hold our children tight to our bodies thinking, *Lord have mercy. I'm so glad I'm not them!* But what we fail to realize is that once upon a time, we were like them.

Once upon a time it took everything you had to go in the church because you knew you smelled like weed or alcohol and you knew you had not showered from sleeping around in the streets last night. But you knew that if you did not go in at that moment, you might never get the chance to get right again.

I decided that I wanted to try to get right with God. I felt like I had hit rock bottom, and by then I was maybe just eighteen years old. I felt like if I could just make it to church, then I would be ok. I could at least start over again.

Then I remembered a church that my grandfather used to preach in when he was living. Even though he had been deceased for a long time by this time, I decided to go to that church. It was a little old-fashioned basement church with a lot of elderly people but I felt I needed the direction of older women. I also attended a close family member's church, because I did not know exactly where I wanted to be. I was still running with my gang and selling drugs and getting high. I guess I thought if I went into a church the urge would just go away and I would not want to smoke weed or hang out with the gang. But it did not work like that.

When the gang found out I was going to church, they became very upset with me. Maybe they thought if I was in church I was going to sell them out. One thing about the devil is, if you even *look* like you may be about to get your life right with God, he will attack you.

I had been involved in a lot of illegal activity with this gang. Many of the members were gun carriers and freely distributed them to other members. I had sold drugs for this gang and I had climbed the "gang ladder" of authority. I held some weight in the devil's camp. I even recruited young boys and girls as new members and had developed a "set" of my own.

I had many rivals out to kill me and it seemed like I had to use that Black & Decker staple gun on someone every time I looked up by this time. At the same time I lived with my mother and I did not want anything to happen to her. We shared the Jimmy truck and at any given moment someone could mistake her for me and just blow it up or something. Many members already knew how to make bombs.

One day, I was driving in a nearby residential area in my Jimmy truck and I saw a beat-up car approaching me. I did not think anything of it, but as it got closer, I saw someone lean out the window holding something. I squinted to get a better look and about fifteen feet away from me someone started shooting. It happened so quickly that all I had time to do was duck and press the gas. I was reaching for my own gun when I heard their tires squeal. As they sped off, I sat up in awe. My front window had been shot up. There were no bullet holes anywhere else on my truck so it was obvious they just wanted to shoot me and drive off. I never found out who they were. I do not know if they were an opposing gang or if it was my own, because there is no brotherhood in Satan's kingdom. Everyone is for himself.

On top of that, I had to go home and tell my mother what happened. When I told her, I just said I had an accident. But after she came to see for herself, I had some explaining to do. We sold the truck right after the insurance paid for a new front window. One would think that incident in itself would have been enough to make me straighten up and fly right. For about four weeks I was scared straight, but after the commotion died down I went right back into that life. I went to the leader of my gang and asked for probation.

Not only was I a reckless church member, but I had become an unruly gang member also. I had done a lot of things the gang considered violations, some so bad the penalty should have been death. You usually cannot get out of a gang once you are a member because you know too much information. The only way out is death. Either you get killed by a rival gang or you get killed by trying to get out of the gang you are in.

I figured if I promised not to let church stand in the way of my gang activity then they would let me be a living member. Then when I got to a certain level and had so many people under me, I could do what is called a "set back," which is basically when you are no longer

When Between Pillars - Push!

out in the field doing dirt. You are the person in charge and people have to do dirt for you. The only time you have to go in the field is when there is a gang war or something really big and drastic. I didn't tell the leader that these were my plans; I just waited for him to accept my idea. He accepted and I walked out with just a beat down and probation. Thank God for that. This time I had one foot in the church.

Tithing in church had never been a problem for me because I had always seen it done in my family. The days my mother did not go to church she would always send her tithes with one of the kids. So I tithed out of habit—and I gave the full ten percent—but it was mostly dirty money from drug sales and the stuff I did in the gang. Only a little of my tithes came from my job. I knew the people who were over the accounting at the church, so I never put the money in an envelope. I never put my name on it. I figured, God is all-knowing and he knows the tithes came from me. That is why it is so important to pray over the tithes and offerings that come into the church. You never know where they come from.

I did not mean to be a hypocrite in church; it just seemed to happen naturally. I would be high in church, sitting in the back on the days I did not sing in the choir. It got to the point where it gave me a headache to hear the Word of God. And on top of that, I had been asked to rap for Jesus. ME? A CHRISTIAN RAPPER? I despised them worse than bad music itself. How could I rap for God when I had been rapping all this time in the world for the devil?

The first time I rapped for God I had two partners and we rapped a song called "Dear God." I sang the chorus: "Now I lay me down to sleep, please don't let him take me. I pray the Lord my soul to keep, don't let the devil break me." I think I heard the words for the chorus somewhere on the street or in some music lyrics and decided it was exactly how I felt.

We rapped and rapped and when I got to my verse I said:

Dear God, sometimes I think I do see demons.

They be sitting at the corner of my wall and they be scheming.

I tried once before to turn the other cheek but they be pointing at me laughing and claiming that I'm weak.

You're the one that beat the devil and be in Satan's dreams, but every time I turn around he's messing with me.

Dear God, I ask you just take him off my back.

Let him know that if he mess with yours he'll get his dome cracked.

And I will watch the way I walk and how I talk,

making sure that your witness isn't outlined in chalk".

I sang that song with everything I had, chorus and all. I was sweating when it was over but I was not ready to change.

I rapped in the church for almost four years. We went around to different churches and rapped. People loved it because I told everything about myself in my music. To me it was an outlet. To others, it was a way to get gossip topics. Incidentally, you cannot share your testimony with everyone because some people are not mature enough to receive it. My songs were basically a cry for help. I did not need judgment; I needed someone to pull me out of the lifestyle I was living. I wished God did not give us all a free will. I wished God just made us obey him. That way everyone could go to heaven because everyone would love God. But God does not want robots. He wants us to love him because we just do, not because he forced us to.

I actually wanted to do right but it was like someone inside of me made me do the wrong thing. Something made me want to sin.

> *For that which I do I allow not: for what I would, that*
> *Do I not; but what I hate, that I do.*
> Romans 7:15

I continued in that lukewarm lifestyle until we did a song called *Confession*. In this song, the guy and I told everything about ourselves in music form and we made ourselves naked before the Lord. For me confession was just a way to expose my conscience to God. I had to actually get high before I could do it, just so I would be numb to the reactions I might receive from the church. The words were as follows:

> I have a confession I been messing with the devil's piece,
> The devil and me don't equal Christianity.
> For three odd years I been eating the devil's feast,

And when I called on my angels they stepped away from me.

Over and over I called the darkness of sin into my grin,

And triple sixes held my life from a limb.

Until the end of time,

I want rewind on my life's tape,

'Cause flags of blue and black be leading my mistakes.

I make extra efforts to go against God's plan,

My wicked mind and thieving hands be on Satan's command.

I try not to lie but my eyes be holding traps,

And though I don't like killing souls my friends carry gats.

My feet be swift and running with mischief on their mind,

And everything I learned in church I leave it behind.

I have backslid more times than Sprint's got dimes.

Have turned lukewarm, from cold to hot,

I been claiming representing but I feel I'm not.

Don't look at me; I'm just the woman that follows the man,

Jacking up God's plans because I take them in my hands.

I'm the spot in the light.

The pain in your contacts,

If the devil saw me trippin' he'd make me sign his contract.

And parents tell their kids to be like me.

If you haven't seen hell, then come spend a night with me

In the dark I toss and turn, in the still of night

Satan sings me lullabies before I say goodnight.

I got tears in my lashes but it's not too late.

Lord, forgive me for my sins and keep my soul straight.

    That was just the first verse. By the time I finished it, everyone was looking at me like I was a demon manifested. I had already been nervous about doing this song. I had so much to confess and my partner's verses were not nearly as bad. Next to me, he was a saint. When I got to the second verse, everyone held his or her breath as I began:

> I'ma be honest for the first time in my life,
>
> 'Cause God is calling me, but I be putting up fights.
>
> I feel bad about my life 'cause I'm up front in the church,
>
> But I'ma say what's on my mind while the weed got my eyes burnt.
>
> I can't see you, but I can feel your eyes on me,
>
> Remember 'The pressures following Christianity'?
>
> That's not just a song with a phat beat for you to clap,
>
> I'm warning you because I fell in that trap.
>
> I'm a soldier that infiltrated
>
> A Christian casualty that just barely made it.
>
> And I confess before the church while my mind's diluted,
>
> I should be booted.
>
> God please save the people I've polluted

If you look into my eyes you'll see I'm ashamed,

I'm a Christian, who liked the look of the devil's game,

I've got lust in my mentals and Trojans in my pants,

I had a fling with Satan when God was my romance,

I pocked my last chance for salvation,

And then sold it to the gang's nation for probation.

I can't go back in time to undo what I did,

I chose this path of life 'cause I'm attracted to sin

It's no wonder why I see demons,

They know me by name.

God take me out of hell, In Jesus' name.

Awestruck could not begin to describe the look in the eyes of the audience. I had a complex already when I rapped, because when my partner rapped everyone would be clapping and dancing, but when it was my turn to rap you could hear a rat pee on cotton. It was *that* quiet. Everyone's eyes would be fixed and the whole audience would lean in like they did not want to miss a single word. I stood up, relieved. I felt like a huge weight had been lifted off my shoulders and I did not have to pretend I had it all together in Christ. I had just told God and everyone in the church how un-together I was.

> *If we confess our sins, He is faithful and just to forgive us our sins, and to cleanse us from all unrighteousness.*
> I John 1:9

That confession was the beginning of my really wanting to make a real effort for God. I did not have the weight of all those secrets on me. Confession is good because as long as we keep something to ourselves, it gives Satan the advantage to use guilt against us. It is at those moments, when we are weighted down with choices and pretending to be good Christians and knowing we are not, it is then Satan comes to put the cover of guilt on us.

What if the church finds out you did drugs? Was a prostitute? What if they find out you slept with the landlord to get an extension on your rent? What if they find out you used profane language? What if they find out you are a closet alcoholic or you beat your wife? They will kick you off the deacon board. They will not let you preach if they find out you went to jail for murder. They will not let unwed mothers sing in the choir. They are not going to let you start a deliverance ministry because you previously ran numbers. Satan says all these things to us when we keep secrets.

> *For there is nothing hid, which shall not be made*
> *Manifested; neither was anything kept secret, but*
> *That shall not be known and come abroad.*
> Luke 8:17

So what if they find out what you used to do! The person you sit next to at church has probably done worse than that. This is why it is good to confess. We have enough attacks from the devil and our own flesh. Why add to it by harboring secrets God knows anyway?

> *Confess your faults one to another, and pray one for another,*
> *That ye may be healed...*
> James 5:16

Notice it said to confess *your* faults, not someone else's. Sometimes we tend to focus so much on things that have been done to us, we forget we have done things to others as well. We all need prayer. Pray for one another. Do not *prey on* one another. Exercise the wisdom that God has given you. As noted, you cannot tell everyone everything because some people are not mature enough to receive the truth and they will try to eat you alive. Cannibals and Christians are the only folks who tend to eat their young and slay their wounded. I have seen it in the church many times.

When we confess our faults, the masks come off. Praying for each other makes us focus on encouraging someone other than ourselves. It gets us to pray for the needs of someone else and gets us out of the "gimme-gimme" prayer rut we can sometimes get in. When all this is done, the healing can flow and we can be healed. We can then get up from our knees with a different attitude than before. We can feel like our prayers actually reached heaven. The weight will be lifted because we have made Jesus our burden bearer, our secret keeper and our comforter.

The rap ministry was taking off and the Lord was delivering me through my own lyrics. I talked about things in the songs I wrote that were totally biblical, almost verbatim and I *knew* that I only knew two or three Bible verses by heart. That could not have been anyone but God giving me revelation through the Holy Spirit.

I was getting on the right track. I still had a lot of work to do but at least I was doing my part. I brought everything to God. I had made myself bare. As soon as I had done that, the whole church watched my every move. I could not go to the bathroom alone. Someone was always in my face smiling, and talking bad about me behind my back. Although I did not hang out with anyone in particular, my name was always in the midst of some mess. If it was missing, broken, done wrong, evil or unnecessary, my name was usually attached. And, for once, I was innocent of these things.

But that's how the devil is. Whenever you are growing in Christ, he is all over you! Especially if you were one of the chief sinners or someone he could guarantee a sin from. Just as the ministry started to get good, my rap partner decided I was not living good enough to rap with him about God. His exact words were, "You're not living right." I was shocked. If he was going to dump me with an excuse like that, why did he not do it before I started to get my life together? I had cut down on everything, drugs and all. I had started taking everything to God in prayer instead of handling stuff on my own. I had committed no burglary nor gone to a gang meeting in months. I even gave my Black & Decker staple gun to my mother and told her I was never going to use it again—and *now* he tells me I sin too much! What was up with that?

Since he wanted to split up, instead of looking for another partner, I decided I did not need a partner. I would rap solo. Sometimes God wants to get you away from people, not always because they are bad, but because he needs to talk to you alone. I actually did better rapping alone than I did with a partner. I had free expression and the Holy Spirit could do whatever He wanted. When my ex-rap partner heard me rap for the first time alone he made no comment. Everyone else expressed appreciation and encouragement. He didn't so much as acknowledge my existence. That was odd because we were so close to one another.

After a while of rapping solo, the church decided I wasn't going to rap any more. They put me in the midst of some affair that was alledgedly going on with two members in the church, one of whom, we later found out, was married. One member tried to imply I hooked the two up and the pastor of the church, who was also a member of my family, was ready to lay blame. I said to myself, *When would I have time to hook up two people that are twice my age? I can't hook myself up. How could I make two adults sleep together or kiss or whatever it is they are accusing me of doing?*

The elders, my mother and the pastor all were in a meeting, along with the two adults who had the affair. To this day I do not know what went on because I had not done anything to begin with. All I know is that the Pastor was intent on making this my fault. The two adults were acting like if they said anything, yea or nay, I was going to put a hit out on them and the elders were wishy-washy as to who they wanted to believe.

I could not take any more nonsense. If this is what church is about, send me back to the streets. I could find more loyalty and brotherhood in a crack head than I had found in church! I grabbed my stuff and announced my departure. The pastor yelled at me, saying I could not go because he had not dismissed us. I waved him off, saying I did not have to take this. My mother stayed to continue discussing the situation.

I had done nothing and yet the pastor, who was my flesh and blood, and all the other people were willing to pin all this evil on me. I jumped into my car and headed for the nearest liquor store. *Forget church, I'll never go to another church again,* I thought. *I can get this kind of backstabbing in the streets!* I drank and smoked that night until I was numb. I drove all over the city looking for trouble that night. I plotted to just blow the entire church up with everyone in it. I bought hard drugs. I did not know what I was going to do with them. I was almost angry enough to try them, but the looks on the faces of all those I had served drugs to in the past stopped me. I decided to hustle up some young guys straight out of high school and let them sell it for me.

In other words, I did a complete 360-degree turn-around and was back where I started from in a matter of moments. My faith could not take adversity. In the gang, when you come up against adversity, you just eliminate him or her. But how do you eliminate a whole church?

> *As a dog returneth to his vomit, so a fool returneth to his folly.*
> Proverbs 26:11

I stayed out of church for a little over a year. I began working a better job and I moved to a hideout apartment in the city. It was easier to do "business" out there than in the suburbs. I was balancing my job and illegal activity well. I had a live-in boyfriend, who only helped me get into more trouble. My best friend was a homosexual who loved to shop, go to plays and dress me up. We would play-fight over men when they came into the shop. My mentality was *You're my best friend but what guy would choose you over me?*

For the most part, guys would ask me out to a company dinner or such. Every once in a while my friend would get a date, too. He always dated the guys I wanted. The ones who had beach houses in St. John's and yachts. Those who loved to go dancing and wanted a partner to stay home because he would provide everything with the old money that had been in his family since the beginning.

This guy and I would gossip and I would use him as a priest. He was a heavy Catholic. I would confess to him and he would give advice and atonement in prayer. (He was always saying "You need Jesus, honey.") I loved this guy. He was so nice to be around and he lived just down the street from me.

One day we got a new receptionist at our job. She looked vaguely familiar but I could not remember from where I knew her.

Later I found out I had met her at the park one day when the church I was attending then had a Feed the Homeless day. I had been playing the drums as a substitute drummer in the church band when this little girl on roller blades came up to me saying she knew how to play also. She was in awe to see a woman drummer. I later found out she talked about me a lot on their ride home that night. I offered her the sticks because I just wanted a break. I had been craving a beer and our guitarist had already blazed a blunt in the middle of praise and worship. (Man we were messed up!) But she was afraid to take them so I had to wait until our normal drummer arrived.

At any rate, the receptionist at my job turned out to be the girl's mother. She was on fire for God and determined she was going to get me saved. Even after I had told her everything about me, she was still on me like some sort of Jesus freak! (Now I know that there's nothing wrong with being a Jesus Freak, but then I was like, HANG 'EM ALL.) We developed a work-related friendship and soon she started inviting me to dinner. I hesitated on taking her up on the offer until later on.

Lukewarm

I cannot remember if it was she or my mother who begged me to go to church the next Sunday, but I finally decided it had been a real long time and everyone probably forgot about the stuff I had been blamed for. I "snuck" into the church wearing two afro-puffs, a long afro-centric black skirt and a brown shirt that looked like it was vintage. Not to mention some plastic beads around my neck. I sat in the back next to my ex-rapping partner's girlfriend and pretended not to notice that everyone had noticed my entrance. I saw the girl from work and several cousins of mine and the little girl I met at the park and *Good Lord, who is **that**?* He was sitting next to the little roller blade girl and he was handsome to me. He was light skinned and cleanly shaven; he had an even haircut that had curls and he had on the brightest orange windbreaker I had ever seen. I stared at him until he felt the heat from my eyes and looked back with a frown on his face. I smiled at him, but he turned his face from mine.

I stared at him all through church. You know how when someone thinks you are cute, they stare at you; but when you look at them, then they look away? Well, I did not look away. I had developed an attitude over the last couple of years that if I saw it and wanted it, be it man, money or anything better, I just took it because there was nothing I could not have. And I wanted him.

When church was over, I hugged everyone, including the receptionist from my job and her daughter. That is when she introduced to me the guy I had been staring at all through service. He was her brother and he was already generating a fan club from all the ladies in our age bracket. I side-glanced him and mumbled a hello. I didn't want everyone to know I was crushing on this guy. I knew people who had made it their personal mission in life to try to take whatever I was going after, be it a man or anything else. He rushed for the exit, pursued by all the ladies. I wasn't going to chase him because I figured that if his sister and I hit it off she would eventually 'put me on' with him. If not, oh well...

I supposed he was running from all the girls because, just as I was exiting the church, he was entering and he almost ran into me. I took that opportunity to make my move. I looked him straight in his eyes and asked him for a hug. He looked confused and when he gave me a hesitant hug I said, "Don't you ever leave this church again without hugging me." It was not a threat. But I said it flirtatiously. I found out later the reason he was running from everyone was because they were telling him not to associate with me because I sold drugs and was in a gang and was a bad person. But I did not look that bad to him. I did not have that "thug" look about me. I did not have razor marks and cigarette burns on my face like the other females who ran in gangs. And all the bad talk just made him want to know me more.

Our friendship did not start out great either. We found out that our gangs were rivals and after church while we were smoking cigarettes, I would throw up disrespectful signs about his gang on his chest, just to see what he would do. But he was a lot calmer than I was. When I went to dinner over to his sister's house and he was there, I would use every disrespectful name I knew in talking about his gang. I wanted to see how do-or-die he was, because I still wanted to get with him, and I wanted to see if his gang affiliation would make him hesitant about getting with me.

What *was* slowing us down was his sister and her husband. I had a cousin that was into this guy deep and every time she would come over they would leave the two of them alone to do whatever. But when I came over they would not let us be alone for two seconds.

When Between Pillars - Push!

If I spent the night and they went to bed at nine, I had to sleep in the room with the rollerblading girl at nine. When my cousin spent the night, if they went to sleep, they would just let her hang out with this guy all night. It was obvious the same people who had talked to this guy I liked had talked to his sister and her husband also.

Nonetheless our friendship grew until he decided he was having feelings for me and he wanted to be my man. We made an agreement that as long as we were going out we would not let the gangs come between us. I did not have any problem doing that. I was almost at "set back". What I *did* care about was the list of demands this guy had. He blatantly told me that when I was with him I could not sell any drugs. I had to go to church and I had to do strictly legal activity. *Hypocrite!* I thought, *Don't you run with a gang too? You know how unpredictable it can get. It ain't that easy.* But I just looked him in the eye and said, "I can do that."

We went out, hung in the city, met his friends; and we would go out to eat every time we went out. But he had a curfew. We were nineteen or twenty then. He had to be in by 10:30 p.m. or 11:00 p.m. depending on his sister's mood. That was a let-down. I had not been out with a guy who had a curfew in my life. Sometimes he would lie and say he could come in late, but then when I would bring him home, he would be trouble. Once, he was on punishment from me for almost a month. He could go out with anybody else if he wanted to. The punishment only applied to going out, calling or associating with me. It was really a ploy to keep us apart. Everyone wanted to see him get with my cousin. But we wanted to be with each other too much. It only made our relationship stronger.

CHAPTER FIVE

Demons? In The *Church?*

A lot of people want to know if you can be a Christian and still have demonic forces try to inhabit you. My answer is *yes,* you can. To understand whether a Christian can have a demon try to inhabit him or her, we need to know what a demon is. I have not read in the Bible where anyone called a demon by the name demon, but they were called devils. The term "devil" means an evil spirit, fiend, demon. It's also defined as Satan, a wicked or cruel person, a very clever, energetic or reckless person, an unfortunate person and an evil influence or power.

When Between Pillars - Push!

Careful study of the Gospels will show you there are many kinds of devils by which people can be possessed. We already know some of the obvious: devils of lust, stealing, jealousy and every evil thing we can think of. But there are also some not so obvious devils. Some are devils of self abuse found in Mark 5:2-6, devils of being dumb as found in Matthew 9:32-33 and Luke 11:14, and devils of being blind found in Matthew 12:22. Those can be found in any person. An infirmity that will not let up could be a devil because it is of an evil influence. But with the Word of God, devils have to leave.

I believe that Christianity is the belief in Jesus Christ. We say that Christ is, was, and always will be a *living* part of the Trinity; making up God the Father, God the Son, and God the Holy Ghost. Jesus died on the cross for our sins. He was buried, and after three days rose for our salvation. When he ascended up to heaven, he sent us a Comforter, in the Holy Ghost. All we have to do according to Acts 16:31 is believe on the Lord Jesus Christ, and we will be saved.

Your belief in Christ deals with your heart. Whether you have old baggage from before you accepted Christ or a devil of anger or any other evil spirit inside you, or even on you, depends on where you have been, what you've been involved in, who you have opened yourself up to and even who you have slept with. When you sleep with someone you become one flesh. So if *they* have a devil of lust, perversion, foul language and other things not of Christ in *them*, guess who *also* has opened the doorway for it? It is expected to be able to pass evil influences in the world, but those influences can also be passed in marriages and in the church. All it takes sometimes is one Jezebel spirit to hook up with someone fresh in the Word, or weak in the spirit and the evil spirit spreads to others.

Have you noticed people who have Jezebel spirits, seducing spirits and even familiar spirits are the ones always volunteering to be prayer partners? (*Oh, we've seen them.*) The sister with the skirt clear up to her belly button and tight as saran wrap always wants to pray for someone or with someone alone. It is not to say she does not believe in Jesus or accepts him as her savoir; but that the spirit she is carrying prevents the breakthrough of God. Also, if you study Luke, Chapter 4, you'll find spirits know they can be cast out in the name of Jesus. So, if they can distract you during prayer, your words will not flow forth and their job is done.

After a while, my boyfriend's sister got permission from the pastor of our church to start a deliverance ministry. It started as a Friday Night Live kind of thing. We would all sit in a circle and have a huge Bible Study and afterwards we would eat snacks that were set up for us to socialize and mingle. I was not going to go, but she said there would be food. That made it sound inviting. (Ya'll know how some of us are: we won't come to church on any day of the week except on Sunday, unless there is food.)

The first time I attended I spent most of the time ignoring the study and thinking about the food. After all, there was only *she*, my boyfriend, four other people and myself. All they were talking about was the stuff God had delivered them from. When it was over I was the first one at the table to eat. That is when she came up to me and said, "How'd you like it?" She had a huge smile on her face.

I almost choked inside. What was I going to say? I can't stand in God's house and lie. "It was…it…it was…mmmm this food is good! Who made the dip? "I totally changed the subject.

She nodded like she already knew what I was thinking, "I expect to see you every Friday."

WHAT? Friday's are the best days to be on the block because everyone gets paid that day and they're ready to smoke their paychecks up! I knew I had promised her brother I wouldn't sell any drugs or do any illegal activity, but by this time I had people who did all that stuff for me and all I did was get paid. "I don't know if I can come every Friday," I told her. But then she challenged me, asking what I had to do that was so important. And I never *did* make a practice of lying. I'll keep a secret forever, but if I'm put in a situation where I have to lie, I won't speak at all or I'll tell it all without tact. I chose the silent route. "I'll be here."

The Friday Night Live started to actually get live. In almost four weeks time the group had gotten so big that people could not sit in the circle and people from churches I had never heard of were coming in. One night, she invited a minister whom she knew and he was really into the deliverance thing. We all were sitting in rows by then. He passed out a piece of paper and explained his ministry and how he prayed for people to be delivered from different demons. Now I know a lot of people do not believe in that kind of stuff, but I do, because I have been on both sides of the fence. We all were supposed to repeat after him a simple prayer that went something like, "Dear Lord Jesus, I accept you and I believe you can heal me. I ask that you forgive me for harboring anger against [you were supposed to whisper the person's name] and I ask that if there is anything not like you inside me that it be bound in Jesus' name." Then he asked us to read the paper, which had printed on it a list of emotions and demonic influences that were jealousy, envy, greed, murder, homosexuality, etcetera. He told us to say, "If any of these things are in me I ask that you take them out, in Jesus' name. Amen."

I thought, *This is deliverance? I still feel the same.* But he was not finished. He went up to each one of us in our chairs to anoint us with oil. He said, "In the name of the Father, Son and Holy Ghost." I watched him touch each person and when he touched my forehead with the oil, I frowned. It burned! I had never had oil burn me. I smacked his hand away. I suppose since he had done this before, he knew what to watch for because he looked at me, and I could hear him say to one of the other ministers, "You see what's happening here? I felt like I was in a tunnel and his hand was still on me with the oil burning like acid. I heard myself tell him not to touch me and I smacked him again. He did not touch me from that point forward. He just started praying in plain English to Jesus and I felt a dizziness come over me as the demon overtook me. This demon came up swinging! (From this point I have to believe what onlookers told me because I was not even there.)

The demon took complete control. I was kicking and I almost hit the minister in his face as I flipped backward attempting to get away from him. I kicked the chair up and on the way down, a couple of men tried to restrain me, but I had thrown them off me. The minister who had anointed me with the oil commanded the demon to be still in the name of Jesus. All the while he had been calling this thing out of me and it was having a fit of rage. Only because he told it to be still in the name of Jesus it obeyed and I came to myself. I was lying on the floor with four full-grown men and several others holding me down. My forehead still burned from where the oil had touched me.

He looked me in my eyes and said, "Meka, you've got to let this thing go." *I'm trying*, I thought. "Say, Jesus Save Me," he commanded. I tried to say Jesus' name, but it felt like something was clamping my mouth shut! I could only make a *J* sound. "I can't," I cried. "It won't let me." I was overtaken by dizziness again. The demon had surfaced again. They went at it for over an hour with this thing. It told its name and everything. It told who else in the room was carrying a demon, and in a fit it tried to rip me up inside. When it could not stay any longer, I felt something crawl up my throat and I started to gag and choke. They rolled me over and I coughed until I felt the thing leave my body.

When I finally came to myself, the ministers were on the ground, the room had cleared, and everyone was covered in sweat, including myself. I found out later that everyone the demon pointed out had been delivered. I was sore for a week. I slept until the next Friday Night Live.

By the next Friday, everyone had heard about what happened the week before and it was packed with folks who wanted to be delivered. This was even the pastor's first attendance at one of the deliverance sessions. The deliverance minister did the same thing as the last week, only this time we were in a circle and for some reason the pastor was standing behind me. *I hope I don't have another demonic episode,* I thought. *At this rate, I'll have to quit the church because everyone's going to think I have demons.*

This time he did not even have to touch me. The words alone that we prayed made anger rise up in me. *Oh great! Please, God, don't let me get delivered now.* I looked up at the pastor behind me and I heard myself say, "If you don't get away from me, I'll kill you." I saw his eyes widen in shock as the dizziness overtook me. They recognized quickly that that demon was trying to manifest because he tried to grab the pastor and the minister of deliverance. The demon also told on everyone who was possessed in the room because they could not get those spirits out of me while the other demons were around. It was as if they were feeding off each other. Once we all were separated from each other we all were delivered.

After that, there was one last Friday Night Live and everyone was demon free. Halleluiah! Then the pastor decided not to have any more Friday Night Lives. I guess God was only doing something in that season with the group. I do know for sure that after that, I had no more affiliation with my gang. (I had reached set back.) The urge to sell drugs was gone. I told everyone to just keep the money. I did not

When Between Pillars - Push!

want it. I felt so light, so free, that I flushed all the drugs I had hidden for a rainy day down the toilet.

CHAPTER SIX

Still Not Ready

Good understanding giveth favor; but the way of the transgressors is hard.
                                                    Proverbs 13:15

My boyfriend and I continued to go out for a few months, but he kept saying his curfew was one thing when it was another. There were also things going on between he and his sister's husband that caused them to get very heated at one another. After several fights with his family, they ended up kicking him out and he moved in with me.

That same week, we took in his homeless best friend and my younger cousin. The four of us were like the black sheep. Since I was the only one with a steady job, poverty smacked us in the face quickly. The thought of selling drugs again crossed my mind more than a few times. But I actually felt guilty thinking those thoughts, so I decided to just keep it legal. Meanwhile, depression set into the four of us and we all became weed heads.

For food, my younger cousin and I would go into the local food banks or shelters and they would give us enough food for the month. I had gone through three cars and finally we were without one. We had to carry loads of food from the food bank to our home that was at least two miles up the biggest hill in history. This hill was a few concrete slabs short of being stairs. We were two months behind on the rent and when we did pay it, we only paid half. The one bedroom apartment that was beautiful when I moved in was almost bare and looked more and more like a dump. We had sold everything that could be sold to the nearby pawnshop to make ends meet. A week or so later it was burglarized and soon after that it flooded twice. There was water up to our ankles everywhere. When the landlord came to vacuum with the wet-vacuum, he did not do a good job and we were constantly scrubbing mold off the walls because of the moisture and humidity.

In addition, we all took turns being detained by the police. Old capiases we had each forgotten about came back to haunt us. What little money we had went to bail out each other. Then we started to fight among ourselves and if one got money, he/she would horde it. With food and whatever else we got our hands on the same thing would happen.

Finally I got a car and one day we decided to leave the dump and go over to a family members' house to visit. When we got there no one was home, so we sat in the car smoking cigarettes and waited for them to get home from church. I suppose we looked like thugs. My hair had been freshly corn rowed. I had a blue fatigue rag covering the braids so the sun would not burn my greased parts. I should have known something bad was going to happen because there was an old lady outside who made a big spectacle of pulling her car into the garage and locking it up. Ten minutes later the police arrived.

They sat behind us until two other cop cars came. Then they walked up on the car. "Which one of you is Meka?" they asked.

I was looking like, *What do they want me for?* I had done so many things in the past that there was no doubt in my mind I would be arrested. The question was on what charge? My younger cousin, eager to assist, pointed me out. "What's up?" I asked puffing on a cigarette. I gave the area a quick surveillance. They had the vehicle cameras on me and everything. The cop asked if I knew I had a capias and I told him, "No." He informed me I would be arrested for missing a court date for a ticket and I stood up without him asking me to. "Can I finish smoking my square first?" I asked, relieved it was only a ticket. His answer was a firm "No." So, I inhaled one more time and kissed my boyfriend. I put my arms behind my back and just as they were putting me in handcuffs my family members pulled up with their two young children in the backseat.

The scene turned sour quickly with my cousin-in-law demanding an explanation for my arrest; and the police not willing to give one. The whole scene looked like a bad movie. It was full of drama as the police shut the door on me and drove me away.

It was a very quiet ride to the local police station and when we got there they filled out the regular police reports. It was a Barney Fife kind of station with one of those cells that looked like it belonged in Mayberry. I was craving a cigarette. It got even worse when I thought about actually being locked up in there. These cops looked like former KKK members too. *I could be locked up in this jail and they could kill me and nobody would know,* I thought. I asked the cop for a cigarette. He laughed at me and said, "This is a smoke free environment." Yet I could see his partner smoking in the garage. I yelled for a hit of his cigarette but he was not sharing. The cop filling out the report wanted to know nicknames, aliases and tattoos. *What person in their right mind would tell all that information?* I thought.

I sat there for an hour before I overheard anything about where I would be sleeping that night. They had called another district and no one came to pick me up. Finally the cops got angry and were arguing between themselves. One of them said, "If they won't come, let her go, and then they can pick her up on the street!"

Any person without police experience would have jumped at the opportunity to be emancipated, but I had too many run-ins with the law to fall for that trick. What usually happens when they let you go is, when you get picked up again you have the original charge *and* resisting arrest. Nobody said it was fair; it is just how it happens. I voiced my opinion even though nobody asked for it. "Why don't you drive me to the District 1 Station or the District 3 Station nearby." I was trying to get to a station where there were more minority cops and the cells did not have bars. They pretended to ignore me, but they ended up calling another district to pick me up.

The other district sent a petite female cop to pick me up. She, however, yanked my cuffed arms around and pushed me into her cruiser, not caring that I could not fit my feet in the back seat. I started squirming to fit my feet in, *This is the smallest cruiser I've ever been in*, I thought. I gave her a hard time as well. I talked and talked in the back of her cruiser. We passed a new jail that was being built and I quizzed her as to why would she even bother to add another body when they were already overcrowded. She told me to shut up several times but I just kept on talking. After all, nobody had read me my rights before I had been arrested.

When we finally got to the Justice Center I was questioned about my mental state and my allergies and then I was thrown into a holding cell. There was a little old lady about seventy years old being detained for opening fire on a group of teenagers, and a whole bunch of rough looking girls and prostitutes and a *big* Amazon girl with choke marks on her neck and dirt stains around her clothing. I found out later that she had been fighting the arresting officers and had to be maced. She obviously frequented the Justice Center often because when she saw me she appeared shocked to see a new face. She stared at me in a manner I didn't approve of and the silent tension mounted until the atmosphere became uncomfortable for everyone in the holding cell. I was removed for questioning about my mental status. The questioning officer asked me if I felt suicidal and I told her I didn't feel like I would kill myself as much as I felt I would hurt someone else. (I had the Amazon girl in mind.) The officer deemed me a threat to the other prisoners.

I wasn't a threat, but the officers had just assigned I.D. numbers and that determined where we were going to sleep. What if the Amazon girl's number was close to mine and we ended up sharing

When Between Pillars - Push!

a cell? I did not want to think about waking up with that Amazon chick standing over me ready to molest or rape me. And I didn't want to share a cell with any other lunatic either. So I tried to make sure they would send us to separate cells.

They *did* separate us and then they took me into a room and made me strip down so they could search for hidden drugs. "By the way, if we find any drugs on you and you've already made it to the Justice Center, you know that it's a felony, right?" the officer informed me while laughing.

Thank God I did not have any on me. If they find drugs on you in the street, depending on how much it is, it is usually a misdemeanor. *Why hadn't I been searched when they put the cuffs on me, before I got to the Justice Center?* They took my undergarments, because they felt I could choke someone with them, and gave me some loose county jail pants, a county shirt and they took my shoes because of the laces, and gave me a pair of blue medical slippers made from foam with smiling faces on them. The slippers were a size 10 and were too small. So, they gave me the men's slippers. I remember I was having my menstrual cycle that night and I requested sanitary items, but they told me to use toilet paper until the jailhouse nurse came to do rounds. *How will I hold it up? Ya'll have my underpants!* I thought.

I found myself on the psycho wing of the jail that night. The covers were cut up burlap sacks and they smelled of urine. The window was only four inches tall and you could hear the whispers from the floor upstairs where the schizo-psychos were late into the night. They did not just whisper either, they had a sickening, high pitched, I've-lost-my-mind whisper. Their laughter made you feel like a crazy demon was sitting right next to you breathing down your neck. After a couple of hours I began to act crazy, even though I was not. I sat on the desk in my cell all night and stared at the guard post, buzzing the buzzer and not saying anything in it. I was glad when I got out of there.

Fortunately, my mother had me out by the next morning. When I returned to my house that day, I was not the same. I was fed up with everybody. I would find any little reason to kick someone out. *All this time I've been helping these cats and when I get locked up my mother bails me out!* I was livid! But that is how it is when you go out in the world. You spend all this time running the streets and doing all sorts of crazy stuff and when something happens to you, your friends are not there for you. Your mother or grandmother always has to get you out of trouble or family members have to help you out.

When I returned to where my boyfriend and cousin were, we argued for weeks. I felt I had given so much and did not get anything back when I needed it. Soon, my cousin turned on me for her man. And the same night I ended up kicking out my boyfriend. They all got into a taxi and left. I immediately called my brother and we moved everything that was salvageable out into my mother's garage.

When, after a couple of days, I came back to my apartment to make sure all of the trash I had cleared was gone, I found my boyfriend, whom I had kicked out, was still there. I asked what happened to his boy and he told me he would not let him stay with my cousin and him. It did not surprise me because I thought they had always been selfish, especially his boy. He had been walking around the streets for several nights with no place to sleep, so he had come back. It broke my heart. I may have kicked him out, but I was not cold and I still liked him. So I said he could stay until the landlord changed the locks. *Then we both would be homeless.*

When the landlord officially kicked us out, he went back to the neighborhood where his boy lived and I went to a relative's house to rethink my whole situation. *How did I get so low? What am I going to do?* I reflected back to when money was not an issue. I basically lived in my car and took showers at family members' houses. Most people would have gone home to their mother, but I did not want to hear my mother's mouth. I had vowed when I moved out of her house that I would sleep in the park before I came back. Not because she was mean, but because in her house I always felt edgy. Every morning something was left undone and she was yelling about it. I did not want to wake up like that every morning. It was her way or the highway. It was her house. We were allowed to have opinions and all, but when it came to something I really wanted to do, I always had to baby-sit my youngest sister or take one of my siblings with me. I wanted to be alone. I wanted to call my own shots. And if bad things happened to me, I just counted it the price to pay for freedom. Stupid, huh?

Well, my boyfriend and I ended up living with my cousin and her man in the "Hood." We lived in a roach infested, dusty, abandoned, low income housing apartment for two or three months. We slept sitting up and fully dressed on the couch because we never knew when the low income housing people would come in and haul away the furniture left by the tenants who had abandoned it. We were blessed that the utilities even worked because the bills had not been paid in almost half a year. Yet we had heat in the winter, lights, a working gas stove and oven and water. We just did not have much money or food. We would call up different restaurants and pretend they had messed up our order, and the order would always be big because they could mess up a big order easier than a small one and we needed enough food for all of us. We did that to Mexican restaurants, chicken restaurants, pizza places…anywhere it worked. And on buffalo wing night, we made a killing. Some restaurants would not give us the food, but they'd give us a refund. It didn't matter. We were just trying to eat!

I'd make bootleg cab trips in my car to make money, while working at a telemarketing place. When we ran out of restaurants to

Still Not Ready

hit, we started going to the store in the neighborhood. (Every ghetto has a little grocery store that sells fried chicken cheap and sells milk way too high.) We would get fried chicken wings, three for $1.25.

What amazed me was the tenants of this project were all like us: dirt broke. Yet everyone had their hair and nails done the first of the month and everyone had weed and cigarette money, but nobody had food and nobody had goals or ambition or wanted to be anything when they grew up. Everyone wanted to party and get drunk. There were people getting shot over dumb things, domestic violence was the norm and nobody owned or used a washer and dryer. I actually spent a birthday there and all we did was get drunk and high. I was so high I was crawling on the ground across the lot to our door. When I got into the apartment all I could think was *Let me die in my drunken sleep, God. I have hit my ultimate low and I feel there is no way back up. I can never be what I was; I'll always be how I am now.*

When people got evicted, nobody helped. Everyone just ran to see what furniture they could take for their house. The police rode through the projects on bikes and blocked both exits, it seemed, so that no one could escape. In the projects there is only one way in and one way out. The phrase of the day was, "Man, I want to get off of this hill!" The females would sleep with a guy for a joint, and nobody's man had a job! Yet everyone wanted everyone else's man. It was ridiculous! When my boyfriend and I left, it was near Thanksgiving and I was pregnant but I didn't know it because I thought I had lost my baby at four weeks. This was the baby doctors said I would never be pregnant with.

CHAPTER SEVEN

Notice for Testing

We moved to a small apartment, not in the city, but not in the suburbs either. It was a one bedroom and the first thing we noticed was there was no dust or roaches and it had carpet! I almost shouted right there. The leasing agent had no idea from where we came. It did not seem like much to her, but to us it was the bomb! We moved our furniture into it. We went to a local dollar store and bought new clean jogging suits and undergarments and everything smelled so fresh and clean. We showered until we were a shade lighter! It was like we were trying to clean the projects off us. The pastor of the church we used to attend had dropped off a small turkey and dressing, mashed potatoes, stuffing and pumpkin pie. We made a salad and sat down at a little card table on which we had put a tablecloth and some fake flowers, and held hands and we gave thanks to God like we were rich! We had a lot to be thankful for. We thanked him until the food was almost cold. We did not care! He had delivered us from the Hood!

I knew our stay was going to be temporary when we moved in, but my boyfriend did not. He was working little temp jobs and I was telemarketing part-time and together we still could not afford $335 in rent and pay our own utilities and food. I was getting sick a lot and I thought I had the 'flu. I'd run fevers and have headaches. My stomach would be hurting. My bladder. I thought I had a bladder infection because my lower back was always hurting. Then one day I noticed a little puffiness in my abdomen and I figured I was retaining water and it was just symptoms of my menstrual cycle. But the vomiting did not fit. Why would I be throwing up before and after my period? I told my boyfriend one night as he was lying in front of the T.V. and he said, "You're pregnant." *Yeah right, I can't get pregnant,* I thought. I just rolled my eyes and said, "I'm still having my period."

He did not take his eyes off the T.V. "Go to Walgreen's and get a pregnancy test."

"Why am I going to go to Walgreen's and get an eleven dollar pregnancy test just so it can tell me it's negative?" I argued that eleven dollars was too much money, especially when you are hardly making ends meet. He just shrugged and repeated his first statement, "You're pregnant." So I went to Walgreen's that night because I was determined to prove I was not pregnant. I returned with my purchase and notified him I was going to take the test. He remained calm.

I had to urinate in a cup and dip this doo-hickey into it and cover it with a cap. If the test strip changed to a blue line, I was pregnant; if the lines were red, I was not. I did what was required and had to wait three minutes for the results. It remained near the bathroom while I complained about what I could have spent my money on besides that stupid test. He never said a word.

"All right! I'm going to look at the test." I returned to the bathroom. I looked and saw the *blue line.* I gasped in shock. *Oh my*

God! I thought. I grabbed the directions and read them hastily. *I'm pregnant!* I did not know whether to be happy or sad. I then decided I needed a second opinion. All those doctors who said I would not be able to have a baby could not be wrong. I figured something was wrong with the test. I did buy the generic brand and I did not want to get excited, yea or nay, if the test had been faulty. We both decided to go to a free pregnancy clinic and take the test again.

The pregnancy clinic was a Christian outreach clinic in the area. We explained the situation to the lady at the front counter and she prepared me to take a pregnancy test and speak to one of their Christian youth counselors. I took the test and afterwards she escorted us both into the counseling room.

The counselor looked almost virginal. *I can't talk to her; she looks like she's never had sex in her life,* I thought. She smiled warmly at both of us and asked our names, ages and other formalities. "Have you thought about what you will do if you find that you are pregnant?" she asked.

Notice for Testing

What could we do? If she was talking about abortion I could not do it. *I may not be living right, but I'm not trying to guarantee a seat in hell*, I thought.

She clarified, "We don't encourage abortion here, but we do encourage adoption, should you decide that you don't want this baby."

This baby? She was talking as if my pregnancy was definite. She wanted us to really think about deep issues and we did not even know if there was a reason to think or not. I looked at my boyfriend. He seemed as uncomfortable as I. The lady continued talking and then she announced she would get our test results and be right back.

As soon as she left we started talking. I wanted to know what he thought the test would show. I asked what we were going to do and how we would do it. He just repeated, "You're pregnant." *What makes this man so sure I am pregnant? I'm not supposed to be able to have any kids.* I became numb after the woman returned and said, "You are pregnant." I think all the color drained from my face.

By the time we left I had actually gotten used to being pregnant. It was not like it would go away. I realized then I would have to do something I swore I would never do as long as I lived. I was going to have to go back to the hospital.

My emotions were a wreck. All the childhood incidences came flooding back to me. "I don't want to go to the hospital; they always try to keep me," I told my boyfriend one night. "They always want to take pictures and run tests and junk; they treat me like a lab rat!" I was near tears. He hugged me and told me I was older now, and they would not do all that stuff to me because I did not have as many problems as before. That is when we realized we needed insurance. Until then, if it were not a free clinic, then I did not go. Free clinics cannot keep you. They treat you and send you on your way. *Now* we were talking about delivering a baby and free clinics do not do that. I would have to go on welfare.

For those of you who have never had to go on welfare, I hope you never do. But, for those of us who were blessed to have welfare when we needed it, we know it's also one of the most degrading experiences a person can have in life. Even if the people are nice to you and do not treat you like you are a "nobody", your mind still beats you up enough to lower your self-esteem. All I thought as I stood in line with ladies, ladies and more ladies with children hanging onto them crying and their hair all over their heads was, *Did I graduate from high school to be standing in the welfare line? My momma did not raise me to live like this. I could have been somebody. I do not look like these ladies. Look: they LOOK like WELFARE! I don't have eight kids by five different daddies. I have an education. I'm too good for this.*

> *Pride goeth before destruction, and a haughty spirit before a fall.*
> Proverbs 16:18

It was my pride, stubbornness and anger that had gotten me to this point in my life and still I had not learned how to begin to be meek. I still did not get it. God was going to let me keep digging a ditch for myself. He was going to bring me lower until I knew how to bend. That is our problem many times. We do not bend unless he makes us. We do not bow down and worship him unless Y2K hits. (Now, *you* know we were some praying-in-tongues folks on December 31, 1999 at 11:59 p.m.) Why does it always take a federal disaster for us to wake up? His word says, *"EVERY knee shall bow, and every tongue confess that Jesus Christ is Lord,*" so what makes us think we are going to be exempt?

God wants us to have love, joy, and peace, but with it comes long suffering; he desires that we have a spirit of gentleness and goodness to everyone. This is not just people we get along with. Then we would possess meekness, temperance and forgiveness. He said there is no law against people who have these qualities. He wants me to be humble and obey his plan for me. If it requires me to crawl around on the ground, out of my mind like Nebuchadnezzar, his will would be done.

If you are wondering what welfare looks like, then allow me to tell you. Welfare looks like: sitting in front of a person who is too tired to care about your experiences because she has her own problems, and has heard the same sob story from different faces all day long. Welfare looks like: you trading your social security number for $250 a month in food stamps, $115 a month in cash benefits to pay rent and a medical card that half the hospitals do not even accept or acknowledge as insurance. Welfare looks like: one caseworker after another, fighting every month, spending $50 of your cash benefits a month, just to make sure that when the caseworker who *last* had your file quits unannounced (and it happens daily), somebody is willing but maybe not competent enough to try and make sure that your little $115 check is not terminated along with your caseworker. Welfare looks like: you better not be making ANY money on the side by doing hair, cooking, cleaning or whatever it is that you do, because when they find out, they will snatch that little check, those food stamps that are barely feeding your kids, and the bootleg heath insurance. Welfare looks like: they own the check you get from your minimum wage job. Welfare looks like: a catch-22. Welfare looks like: a dead end. Welfare looks like: bondage. Welfare *does not* look like God. Now, if you see something that fits this description in your life, no matter what everyone else says, it's welfare. Rebuke that demon in Jesus' name even before it begins to multiply!

    Once the welfare benefits started, we were definite that we could not afford to live in the current apartment. I could not work because I had morning sickness so bad I could not even drink water. It would come back up. I was taken into the hospital for dehydration so many times I actually got to know the staff. The paramedics knew me on sight. So, when the Lord blessed me with a well day, we jumped at the opportunity to move. Of course, it did not work out immediately as we would have liked.

My boyfriend would stay with friends and I would stay with an uncle until the low income housing place had an opening. I would not normally have been able to move into the low income housing because they needed a police report for you to move in. If you have anything other than speeding tickets, they deny you. You see, people do not always come into the projects messed up and acting like thugs. They become that way if they stay too long. There was a spirit of poverty and murder that dwelled there. God knew I needed shelter for this miracle he was going to do and God allowed the people to accept me.

> *...Can any good thing come out of Nazareth?*
> John 1:46

When I went to sign the leasing papers, the agent was so nice and sweet. She was nothing like the leasing agents I had met before. She explained that the rent was thirty percent of my income (and that was only $115 a month) so the rent was $30 a month. Then she showed me the apartment. It was a two-bedroom townhouse, no carpet, but it had a bathtub and shower (normally, you get only the tub), a washer/dryer hookup; it was a two-level building with a huge kitchen and living room. It even had a front door and back door, plus many closets. It was the largest place I had ever lived in outside of my mother's house. *No wonder people get here and just stay*, I thought.

After a few months I began to feel better and began to have normal hospital visits. I had not gained any weight according to the doctors, but the baby seemed to be growing normally. My pregnancy had begun to grow on me a little and I was beginning to feel all warm and motherly inside. My boyfriend and I talked about names. He was going to name it if the baby was a girl and I would name it if the baby was a boy.

As the doctors were reviewing my old medical records they came across the Klipple Trunany Webber term. Extensive reading of my charts gave them reason to be alarmed. They confided in me that they had never even been taught in medical school of any such thing. So I gave them my hypothesis on my condition and what evidence I had to draw my conclusions on. They casually quizzed me on my medical background, and wanted to know how the disease was affecting me now. What can you say? When you hurt every day from something, you become immune to it. You only feel it if one day you wake up and do not hurt. (I'm still praying for one of those days.)

They gave me a due date of July 12, 1999, because I had still been menstruating up to my fifth month and they usually use the end of your menstrual cycle as the mark to predict the baby's day of birth. That was odd, but not cause for alarm. I had to go in every two weeks because the doctors decided, from reading my childhood medical records and doing some research of their own, I was high risk.

All I thought was, *God, please let me have a boy. I don't want to have to relive my life through a girl. I really couldn't take it. What if she came out messed up like me? She couldn't get comfortable shoes, she'd always have to wear the opaque panty hose, and cute dresses were out! I couldn't deal with myself all over again in another person. I don't know how my own mother took it.*

When they did my ultrasound, I found out that my baby was a boy! I was elated because the Lord had been dealing with me concerning a lot of things. First of all, while every other pregnant lady was craving food, I craved the Word of God like I would die without it. I remember just reading the Bible like it was a good novel!

At this time I started attending church sporadically with my mother at a very fired up church! The first time I went to the church, the praise dancers were skipping around with banners and ribbons. The choir resembled one of those Kirk Franklin choirs and the music was amped! I felt like I had stepped into a Christian Mardi Gras! *If this is what heaven is going to be like, count me in!* I thought.

I remember hearing the bishop of this church say that whatever you called your child could influence what they could become. The tongue had the power of life and death. The members were always talking about *"speaking those things that be not, as though they were."* It works for the positive and negative thoughts. For instance, if you tell a child he is stupid or that he acts just like his absent parent, or that he cannot think, the child may eventually become what you have spoken over him. So, I asked the Lord what could I speak on my son that would be good and he said, *"Uriah"*. I had no idea about Bathsheeba's husband (as recorded in the Bible) or anything, but I had decided to name him what God had put into my heart.

When I looked up the name, it was Hebrew for *God is my light*. Hallelujah! That's what God wanted me to speak on my child. So I started calling him Uriah when he was still in my womb.

CHAPTER EIGHT

The Test

In the last two and a half months of my pregnancy, things began to get odd. It began when they did the ultrasound of the baby. You know how doctors are: a careless "What's that?" and from there on, it is all downhill. We were watching the baby move around and wave when the doctors saw something that looked weird. *I* could not tell by watching the ultrasound but *they* wanted to do an assessment by running a few tests and doing a couple of cat scans. They sent me home without a word but wanted me back within the week.

By the next week I started to have contractions. They connected me to a machine to see how far apart the contractions were. They were too far apart for concern so they gave me medicine to calm them, when and if the contractions returned. In the meantime they assigned one of the best doctors in the city to me because my delivery due date was approaching.

The contractions kept coming, and after weeks of attempting to delay labor they decided to sit down with the father and me, and plan our birthing strategy. A nurse told me I would be signing up for Lamaze classes soon. But plans quickly changed.

The specialist whom they had assigned to me was a short Pakistani woman with dark hair and childlike eyes. According to the tests, she said, there was a big vein in the center of my brain that was the victim of Klipple Trunany Webber. Given my medical history, and the small amount of history the doctors knew about the seven other Klipple Trunany Webber victims, if I attempted to push to have the baby, the pressure of the birth would be too much on my heart and brain. I would run an almost one hundred percent risk of having a heart attack or stroke mid-delivery and die on the table. They would

The Test

then have to hastily cut me open just to save the baby, and my chances of resuscitation would be lessened. I looked at her without blinking and shrugged, "Well, the baby has got to come out."

What else could I say? I was twenty-one years old and the doctor was telling me tactfully that if I had this baby I would die. She told me our next option was a cesarean section and I should plan to have one. I figured it was all good and I could go now, but she wanted to do ultrasounds of my stomach right at that instant. According to her studies of my medical records, during all of my surgeries my skin tissues and blood vessels were like rubber, making it extremely difficult to hold a stitch after I had been cut. Therefore when the doctors would attempt to sew me up after surgery, I would hemorrhage and lose massive amounts of blood.

As I lay on my back they rubbed this jelly residue on my stomach. "I want a bikini cut," I told her, still in the flesh. It had not hit me how serious this whole situation was. I just kept thinking, *I'm already ugly enough; I don't need a hideous scar to add to it.*

She moved around to see how clean the cut would be, "Too many veins," she mumbled distractedly. "We can't cut there; she'll bleed too much," she told the two other doctors who were on her team. "It's going to have to be straight up and down, like an emergency one." They all nodded and mumbled eight-syllable words to each other as she moved the ultrasound scanner to the site where they would cut. She quickly moved to another spot on my stomach and her eyebrows furrowed. They all exchanged worried glances.

"What? What is it?" My eyes were huge as I held my breath. *Please don't tell me my baby is deformed like me.*

She explained that what she was looking for was a clear spot to cut. Everything that looked like the pores in a sponge were veins, which in a normal body did not look like that on the ultrasound. The area where she had hoped to cut usually had few to no veins in the entire region, but as she looked at it on me, it was obvious the veins were woven and intertwined and everywhere. There was literally no place to cut. No way to get the baby out alive. It was a "risk one or the other" situation and still there were no guarantees that the one that *wasn't* risked would pull through.

She looked at the ultrasound of my stomach in black and white and in color on a projector and a small T.V. They started to entertain

The Test

the idea of me having the baby vaginally again, thinking that when I had the heart attack or the stroke they had a fifty-fifty chance to bring me out of it alive. A cesarean was a higher death risk because I would hemorrhage and bleed to death with all those veins. She lubricated the probe to examine my vaginal walls. They were worse than my stomach. Having the baby normally was definitely out of the question.

The question asked was: how will we get the baby out without killing the mother? And they were running out of time, because the baby had decided to poke a pin-hole in the water bag. The contractions were at fifteen minutes apart when I was lying on the ultrasound table. They gave me more pills (Procardia and Breathane) to stop my contractions. Then I was put on bed rest. We did not know exactly how old the baby was. My periods had continued for so long the doctor decided to try to determine the age of the baby just in case they had to take him quickly. She decided to do an amniocentesis. When the results came back they were not great either. "If we can give this baby a few more weeks, he'll have a fighting chance," she told me. *How old is the baby?* I wondered.

Nobody could tell for sure. His size indicated he was big enough to survive, but his lungs were underdeveloped and he could have a difficult time surviving out of the womb. They let me go home, but the doctor gave me her home number so I could call if the contractions worsened.

God, you gotta move something here, I prayed silently. My son's father was upset to tears. He had some issues from his own past, and that night when I needed someone to be strong for me and tell me everything was going to work out, I had to hold him and tell him everything would work out.

"Everyone I love leaves me," he told me. He looked like he would cry and my heart felt for him. I really did not know what to say, so I went to what I already knew.

"When I was born they said I'd die. When I was a little girl they said they couldn't help me; they didn't know why I was having seizures, why I'd just bust a vein and bleed forever. They didn't know why after numerous operations I still had the same problem. They wondered why I only stayed out of a coma when I wasn't in the hospital. They didn't know I had a praying family who had a God who can do anything but fail. I won't die." I looked him in the eyes. "I promise."

How could I look someone in the eyes and tell him I would not die and I did not have any control over whether I died or not? How could I promise him I would make it when I was still living in obvious sin? I am not going to say I had unwavering faith and that my eye was on the sparrow and I prayed and fasted to God and I just knew he was going to let me live. I just knew I was *not* going down without a fight. I had been through too much stuff in my life and I started to believe maybe God did have a purpose for me. Why else had God allowed me to live through all those countless times when I should have been dead and in hell?

I had spent so much time with Satan that I knew his game. It's like your siblings. Nobody knows you better than they do. You know the person you grew up with better than their mother. Why? Because you ran together, got in trouble together, told each other secrets, fought each other until you could smell each other's weaknesses and you recognized the wrongdoings of your brother, his craftsmanship, or the scent in the room. That is how Satan and I were. He was like a sick and twisted big brother—but not anymore.

The first thing the adversary told me was that my entire purpose for living as long as I had was because I needed to have the baby. The baby was going to do something great in the Lord, but I would not. Immediately after I had him I would die because God had no more use for me. Scriptures taunted my mind with all the incidences of death during childbirth. "Did some women in the Old Testament die when they were having their children?" he taunted. I could not remember her name and only pieces of the scripture came to my mind. Something about the child bringing her much sorrow…I tore into the concordance of my Bible to find a key word. I was determined to find that scripture. *Death…death…sorrow…*I thought, leafing through the pages. I spent an hour searching for death and sorrow before even I realized what the adversary had done. He had my total concentration on death and sorrow and it was literally eating me up to find it! *Ok, you got me this time, devil, but you won't do it again.*

This is why it is so important to cast down every thought and every high imagination that exalts itself against God and His Word. The adversary is good at what he does. He had billions of people before us to practice on. He will have us meditating on all kinds of stuff if we do not keep our focus on the Lord. He knew the Word when he tempted Jesus after his forty-day fast. He knew it then and he knows it now. He is persistent. That is why the Word of God says if you resist the devil, he will flee. Resist means to withstand the action or effect of, strive successfully against. Any book that says ignore the devil and he will flee contains a typo or a lie. Ignore means to overlook or neglect. You do not want to ignore your enemy, especially when he is about to attack. His blows will take you unexpectedly and you will fall. If you resist your enemy it means you are fully aware and have your guard up for his attack. This way, when he hits you, you do not fall.

As the weeks went on I ended up spending almost the whole month being shot up with celestone steroids to quicken the development of the baby's lungs, and taking breathane pills and inhalers and magnesium treatments intravenously. I had medical consultations about how they would get the baby out when they could not use an epidural because of the severe curve in my spine. As they wheeled me back to the room, they gave me more bad news. During their studies to determine how I could have the child and live, they looked at the other seven cases of the people having my disease to this severity. They figured that whatever worked for them would work for me. Six of the stricken were men and the one woman who had the disease died having her baby. Doctors had one practice try before me and she had died. I was basically the second try. The six men had not even lived as long as I. The disease had overtaken them at youthful ages. The doctors shook their heads like there was no hope. My mother and several prayer warriors went on a fast on my behalf.

> *And I sought for a man among them, that they should make up the hedge, and stand in the gap before me for the land, that I should not destroy it...*
> Ezekiel 22:30

In a time like this, there was a need for real prayer warriors, not just Sunday only prayer warriors. All prayers to Jesus on the behalf of a person in need are great, but when it comes to fasting, I cannot express the importance of sticking with it. This was not a time for people to be claiming to fast and sneaking snacks at the same time. (You know it happens.) That is why it is important to be obedient in a fast. It is better not to even volunteer to intercede with fasting, than to start and then cheat on a fast. That gives the adversary lead way to attack. (The little fox destroys the vine.) This was not a time to have little foxes nibbling on the vine!

The doctors wheeled me back into ultrasound. Nothing was stopping this baby from coming. They decided they would do a cesarean instead of a natural birth and wanted to take one last look at where they would cut. Maybe something had changed, maybe some veins had moved and they could have a clear site to make the incision. But when we looked, everything looked as it had before. They sighed like "we give up" and motioned aimlessly near my navel. "We'll cut here." They set a date for July 28. This was it. It was crunch time and the odds of winning were grim. *God, just let me live to see my baby; then I can die in peace,* I prayed silently.

CHAPTER NINE

Push!

July 28, 1999, the doctors began prepping me for surgery. They made me sign waivers and a power of attorney. In the event of my demise, they wanted to know who would have custody of the baby. They slipped me a paper to have a tubal ligation. *What's that?* I thought.

I suppose the doctors saw my confusion, because one rushed to explain that if I made it through this delivery they wanted to tie my tubes because they did not want to do this again. They felt like the risk of death was higher with age and right now age was all I had on my side. I was instantly steeped in depression; my boyfriend and I were not married. If they tied my tubes, I would never be able to have a real family with someone else and he could just go on with his life like I never existed. I refused to sign the papers.

That was when he volunteered to have a vasectomy. But the doctor's concern was for *my* future in childbirth. They felt I did not need to take that risk in the future. I cried as I thought about being neutered. I felt like I was an animal. I was only twenty-one years old and I felt like my life was over. I had been through so much in the hands of the enemy and my own hands. It seemed to me that the odds had been against me since birth. My mother convinced me to sign the papers, but I was very depressed entering surgery.

The doctors had called a nearby blood center and had massive amounts of blood reserved, because they knew I would hemorrhage. This is a trait of the disease and I'd had many transfusions as a child. They shaved me and made sure the surgery room was ready. I could not have my baby in Labor and Delivery because the room was not equipped with all the utensils necessary for this kind of surgery. They put the I.V. in each arm, making it possible to replace the expected loss of blood quickly. Every specialist in the hospital was paged and expected to be in surgery. Sixteen other doctors were in attendance. The whole Labor and Delivery shut down. If any other woman thought she was going to have her baby while I was having mine, she would have to do it with a nurse because everyone was prepping for my surgery. None of my relatives were allowed to be present because there was a surety of this being emergency surgery. Everyone prepared for the worst.

I kissed my boyfriend, and I looked at my mother who was breathless by my side. "Who loves you?" she asked. I choked back tears and as the doctors wheeled me away. I said, "Jesus."

When we arrived in surgery, there were already several doctors waiting. They put me on the operating table and strapped me down on my back. They stuck various tubes into parts of my body and put the oxygen mask on me. A masked face asked, "Comfortable?" *How am I going to be comfortable?* I thought, nodding. They turned on the gas and I could hear their voices fade away as my eyelids got heavy. My limbs felt like mush. *Forgive me, God.* I thought. *Remember to let me see my baby.*

Up until this moment the story of Samson meant nothing to me. As a child they always teach you about some guy with brute strength, a strength that resides in his hair, and who can beat anyone. Yet a woman took Samson's strength down and made him weak by the cutting off of his hair. What was so interesting to me was that Samson was blessed by God at birth, but he felt that he was a self-made strongman. Samson blatantly disobeyed the Nazarite vow that said he should not drink wine nor strong drink, he should not eat any unclean thing and no razor should come upon his head (Judges 13:7). Samson was to be God's from the womb until the day of his death. He killed lions and men and destroyed whole armies and he killed thousands with the jawbone of an ass.

Yet Samson did everything he was not supposed to do and fell in love with a foreign woman. Back then, foreign women did not necessarily mean a different race; it also meant a different religion. Be careful of falling for foreign people, people outside of the Christian faith. Do not be unequally yoked with a guy or a girl just because you like him or her, or just because he or she is a nice person, or because he or she helps you with your bills. When you hook up with someone outside of the faith, eventually someone is going to change. (Either you, or them.) And someone is going to compromise what he or she has been taught. And too many times it ends up being the person who confessed salvation openly who gets turned around.

God gave Samson favor regardless of how he was cutting up. God had made a promise concerning Samson even before he was born. God said Samson would be his from the womb until death. So, it did not make God change his mind about the promise he made, just because Samson was not acting right. He still gave Samson strength. You see, humans will promise you something and then take it back. But the God I serve is a non-reneging God. He is not a man that he should lie, nor the son of man that he should repent.

It was only when Samson told the secret of why he was so strong to *his enemy,* while laying in her lap, that he suffered the consequences and was put in the prison to grind. Samson took the blessing of independence and strength and traded it for bondage.

That is what the enemy wants to do with us. He wants us to lie in his lap and get relaxed and tell him our strengths and weaknesses. And we often do by speaking those things out loud. We tell the enemy everything and we do not tell God anything until we have fallen into the enemy's trap. But even though Samson was stripped and shaven and abused by his enemies, it was during that time that restoration began. During this time, his hair began to grow. His strength was being renewed. His relationship with God was reestablished.

Sometimes God has got to let us run wild and fall by the hand of the enemy so we can reestablish our relationship with him. Sometimes we have got to be treated badly to know when we have it good. And sometimes when the enemy has poked our eyes out and we cannot see a thing, it is then we see everything so clearly.

This was a humbling experience for Samson. He had always been so strong and in control of everything. People were making fun of him because he had always done so much better than them and now he was low. This mighty man who could rip a lion in half with his bare hands, and slay champions and thousands of his enemies with a bone now could not even break free from some chains and fetters. He was blind and dependent, and reduced to below average strength. He was now the lowest, dirtiest, most stinking, greasy filthy man they had seen. And his enemy was glad about it.

> *And it came to pass, when their hearts were merry, that they said, call for Samson, that he may make us sport.*
> *And they called for Samson out of the prison house; and he made them sport: and they set him between the pillars.*
>
> Judges 16:25

The enemy wanted to make fun of Samson more. They wanted a closer look at his misfortune to make them feel good about themselves. Their hearts were merry. Everyone had "jokes", as the young kids say. The same with us: we ran with Satan one minute and God the next and then we decided we liked Satan's side better. We say, "They got it going on over there!" The next thing you know, we are in a situation of lack. Why? Because of something we should have done and our decision *not* to stay with God.

But everyone is talking about me! So what! Let them talk! When they talk about you and you are right with God, they put you in a position of blessings, just like they did Samson. They were so intent on making fun of him and doing him wrong that they got the spiritual

When Between Pillars - Push!

"laughing cramps." That's when you laugh so hard your stomach hurts and you have to ball up and hold it. All your concentration goes into making it comfortable again and you cannot do anything for anyone but laugh. They laughed so much they became self-absorbed. They got lazy and stuck Samson between the two pillars that supported the whole building and because he had reestablished his relationship with God, and had humility in his spirit, the building fell and killed everyone at his push. All his enemies died. Had the enemy been thinking, they would have made sure Samson had a haircut every two weeks. But the enemy is so vain that when he causes us to stumble he is so busy rejoicing in the mirror about how smooth he is that he gets caught "slipping", and before you know it, we have the victory. Hallelujah!

When your enemy puts you between two pillars, when they talk about you at your job, look around and see where your desk or office is. Do you sit next to the president and vice-president's office? Do you and the personnel manager get along well? Are others always praising your efforts? *You are between pillars; push!* Do you have someone spreading lies about you in church? Every time you turn around your name is in the middle of a scandal and you have not done anything? Who are you close to? The pastor and his wife? A couple of people on the advisory board? *Those are pillars; push!* You're in school and the kids always pick on you "'cuz she got hair" or "she thinks she's cute". Who are your friends? The president of student council and the hall monitor? You eat lunch with the varsity team? The teachers think you are great. The principal loves you. *They are all pillars, so push!*

What I am trying to get you to see is, that it always looks worse when you are between the pillars. Pillars are the support of the building. The enemy wants you to move out of the way before you can figure out that those are what have been supporting the thing that has you in bondage. He does not want you to know that all it takes is a push to bring the whole house down.

People were talking about me up until my son's birth. Folks who thought they knew me were bad mouthing me and here I was in a situation where they felt like, *That is what you get.* But God had said I would be his until death, just like he said for Samson. I was between pillars, prayer warriors, people of God, and people who loved me.

Somebody is saying, *But Samson died.* I don't want to die pushing. The thing about Samson is that he *asked* to die with his enemies; who knows what may have happened if he did not ask to die. He slew more in his death than in his life. And if you absolutely have to die pushing, wouldn't you rather go like that? You don't want to push because you may lose your job. So what if you *do* push and lose your job? The company may have to shut down because you were the light. When you leave, so does your light. God could make it so nobody they hire is good enough and they have to rehire you. Maybe double your salary, and give you a promotion. We need to always think: *When Between Pillars, Push!*

When I tried to open my eyes after the surgery, it felt as though a Mack truck was parked on my stomach. It also felt like someone had taken a knife with a dull edge and sliced my skin. I felt like I was still on the operating table and I could vaguely make out two dark shadows. *Heaven?* I tried to focus but I could not. All I could do was moan about the excruciating pain I was in. I kept saying "my stomach, my stomach," in a strained whisper. I heard my mother's voice far away urging the doctors to turn up the medicine they had plugged into my arm. "Don't feed the baby," I mumbled. I wanted to breast-feed and I did not want anyone feeding the baby Similac. I thought that if I concentrated on feeding the baby I would come back to myself. I drifted off into unconsciousness.

When I awoke again, I was in the regular hospital maternity room and my mother, boyfriend and cousin were there. If anyone else was there, I do not remember because once the nurse brought my baby to me and placed him in my arms, my attention was all on him. He was so small, 6 pounds 3 ounces. He was looking at me with piercing black eyes. He looked so wise. His little body was so warm and I was overwhelmed and I noticed that his hairline went clear down to his eyebrows. I began to cry tears of joy.

I wonder if he'll have hair like that forever? I thought, trying to picture a young kid with hair all over his forehead. You think about crazy things the first time you see your baby. I was so happy to see him, but I was in immense pain. I fed him for the first time and then I let the nurse take him because I was exhausted. *Thank you, God!* I thought.

Not only had I *not* hemorrhaged during surgery, but I had also been the only person they knew of with such a bad case of Klipple Trunany Webber to survive a live delivery. God had done the unthinkable, the unbelievable, and the humanly unattainable—and he did it in front of the highest paid specialists in the city, their protégés and everyone on staff at the hospital who had heard of my pregnancy. *Two* was a blessed number! This was the pillar I stood between; I had no choice but to trust God and push spiritually and with him I knocked down more walls and stigmas and demonic influences at my most vulnerable time than I had in my life! I was celebrating in my mind, but the battle was not over.

CHAPTER TEN

God Is My Light

The baby slept in a crib in my room. I did not want any mix-ups or stolen baby episodes. I felt like I was too close to having the victory to let the adversary catch me sleeping. The doctors came in periodically to check on how the surgical staples were healing and to take my vital signs. The normal rest time for a cesarean was five days and then they would discharge you to go home. It did not seem like too much was going wrong. The staples looked ok. My stomach was a little hot, but nothing to be too concerned about. By the third day they tried to have me walk around and stretch my muscles a little, so that when it was time to go home I could get around. The pain was so severe that after one minute the nurse decided to lay me down and check my stomach again. It was flaming hot!

She asked if I had started bleeding. I had not, so I said, "No." She called for the doctor, who discovered that for some reason blood had backed up in the area of the surgery. They feared I would start forming clots. If one of those clots should travel into my heart, the situation could be life threatening. *Why does there always have to be so much drama?* I asked the Lord. *Why can't I just have a normal delivery and go home?* This was too eerie for me! But God said, "Wait, I want to show you something."

The nurses came in that day and the next to make sure my legs were elevated and to rub my legs and get the circulation going. By the fourth night I noticed a light cough that resonated in my chest. I tried not to cough because my stomach muscles hurt so badly. I complained to the nurse that when I tried to cough it hurt. She told me to cough with a pillow on my stomach to relieve the pressure. I did that all night and my coughs contained more and more phlegm. It was in my lungs and by morning I had a little trouble breathing. I thought I was getting a cold, but pneumonia had started to set in. My lungs had enough liquid inside them to feel it gurgling heavily when I breathed.

"You've got to keep coughing because if you don't the water in your lungs will suffocate you; pneumonia is trying to set in," the doctor said.

I fought the urge. "It hurts so bad when I cough," I whispered. I was not trying to whisper, but with all the water in my lungs, it did not leave much room to take in air. So when I tried to talk it would come out as a wispy voice.

"Do you want to suffocate?" she asked me. I looked over at my sleeping child. *Do it for Uriah*, I heard in my mind. I shook my head. "I don't want to suffocate."

The nurse and the doctor helped me cough all night long. We were determined to beat the little pneumonia that was trying to set in. One nurse was elevating and massaging my legs to make sure I did not clot. I still had not bled and my stomach had started to swell with the blood in that little amount of time. It was still enflamed, but they figured if they got the pneumonia out of my system, I might still be able to go home.

But on the fifth day I ran fevers. They went into the hundreds at night and caused me to sweat my sheets and shiver. By morning they were gone. The next night it happened again and I was bordering the line of deliriousness. I looked over at my mother who had decided to spend the night in my room to watch my baby. I was adamant about not letting him out of my sight. *C'mon, you can pull through this,* I thought, shivering in my own cold sweat. *Do it for Uriah.* I drifted back to sleep.

The doctors could not figure out why I was running fevers and shivering at night. I had started to spot and that was a good sign. It meant the toxic blood would be leaving my body. The stay that was supposed to last five days lasted fourteen days. They ran cat scans, gave me medicine mixtures, and took blood every four hours to test for toxins, medication levels and other diseases in my body. They brought in specialists who were fascinated at the only woman to survive with this kind of malformation in her body and give birth to a child. They requested to bring in cameras and take pictures of my legs and feet and other limbs. I instantly felt like a child all over again. I constantly had to turn down medical photographers who did all but give me money to take one picture of an extremity. I felt like a lab rat as the fevers continued night after night.

One day a lady doctor came in alone. I looked past her, expecting the usual entourage. None came as she sat on the chair next to my bed. She held her chart very close to her body and she looked into my eyes. She told me of the numerous tests they had taken and that all the tests had come back inconclusive. She rambled on about the various medications I had been taking to stop my fevers and chills and to thin my blood and so on. I did not speak. *What is she going to tell me now?* I thought. *It cannot get any worse than it already is.* Finally she took a deep breath and said, "With the night fevers very high and the chills and the symptoms you have been displaying…we think you may have HIV…"

WHAT!? "No, I don't," I said out loud. There was no way on earth I had AIDS. I had just been tested and it came back negative. "You got me mixed up with someone else," I said, trying to control my hostility. They had poked, pried and pricked me; they had run tests and experiments, begged to take pictures and here is a doctor I had never seen with the usual doctors telling me I had AIDS! I was not going to accept it. I knew every doctor in the hospital, but I did not know her. She said, "Just sign this consent to take the HIV test and we could find out…"

"No! I just took an HIV test and it came back negative, and every HIV test since the time I started having sex has come back negative. I am not taking another! If you want a test then take the blood from the one they took earlier. Test *it*!" I could feel myself getting angry.

She stammered for an explanation. "Its just that so many things are going wrong and we don't know…"

"If you don't know, then say you don't know. Don't come in here and tell me I have AIDS and then ask to take a test! Who are you?" I demanded.

She looked like I had smacked her. Then she said, "I'm a doctor here at the…"

I cut her off again. "I don't know you." Then I said, "You gotta leave my room…" I was standing by then and I said to her,

"Go!" I said this while pressing the button for the desk nurse. She left quickly without a parting word and when the nurse responded to my call I relayed the details of our conversation and the lady's description to her. She had a look of puzzlement on her face and said she knew no one who fit that description. I remembered seeing her nametag and I told the nurse the name on it, but she just shook her head and frowned as if to say no one by that name was on the staff.

What makes it worse was none of the doctors, including my own, seemed to know who the woman was, nor did they recognize the name on her tag. Also, when I had relayed the message the woman had given me concerning my HIV status, all the doctors reconfirmed my negative test. I now believe she may not have been *human*, or *real* to anyone else. I believe it was a demon, or an evil spirit on assignment, come to poison me with death. There are lots of evil spirits in hospitals anyway. Those spirits dwell among the sick and dying. Hospitals can almost be a spiritual gateway for the enemy to attack. For example, have you ever gone into a hospital with a minor problem and by the time they strip you down, put that backless robe on you, and lay you on the bed, you begin to feel heavier? Then they wheel you around in a wheelchair when you insist on walking and the next thing you know, you are having that sick-lazy kind of feeling. Those are spirits. In the beds, on the robes, everywhere!

The enemy was so angry I had made it through that he decided to send someone to taint my blood. Who knows what could have happened if I had let that woman take my blood? She could have used an infected needle and transferred the AIDS virus to me. She could have injected me with some deadly drug or she could have just poisoned my mind into thinking I had the HIV virus and then I would start to act out the symptoms until I did die. But God has a way that is mighty sweet. He made it so I knew every doctor, and when she came I could say, *Jesus I know, Paul I know, but who are you?* Hallelujah!

I ran a fever that night also, but I kept an eye open for that woman. I shook and sweated all night, but I would not let deliria take me like it had the nights before. I wanted to make sure nothing happened to my baby or me. Every time someone entered my room I was fully awake, shivering in my sweat. *I'm going to stay awake*, I thought, *for Uriah*. I would stay like that until the fourteenth night of my stay.

That night I ran a high fever but I did not have any chills, sweats or shakes. I hummed songs in my mind that I had sung when I was a little child in the children's choir. I reminisced on the days when guys still had cooties and people's minds were so innocent they thought sex and kissing was the same thing. I prayed to God for guidance and direction. I asked him what he wanted me to do with my son. How did he want me to raise him? How could I be a good witness for him? How could I face everyone I had left behind? And God told me he had given me the secret while I was in the hospital.

Every time I felt I could not do something, I would look at my son and think, *I'm going to do this for Uriah*. As I mentioned earlier, Uriah in Hebrew, translated, is, "as God is my Light." So every time that I would say that I would do something for *Uriah*, I was saying, *I'm going to do this for God, who is my light!* When it looked like I would suffocate from pneumonia I said to myself, *Do it, for God is your light.* When it looked like I could not make it because I was delirious and shivering in my own sweat, God said I could do it *for he is my light,* and when it looked like I could not stay awake to watch for that demon that wanted to give me death, God said I could *because he is my light.* That was what he wanted to show me.

> *The Lord is my light and my salvation; whom shall I fear?*
> *The Lord is the strength of my life; of whom shall I be afraid?*
> *When the wicked, even mine enemies and my foes, came upon me to eat up my flesh, they stumbled and fell.*
> Psalms 27:1-2

I realized if I trust in him with all my heart, and with everything I have and am, and I do not try to figure out his every move or figure out "how Lord, how?" he'll direct the path he has set for me to take. The blood was flowing normally and the staples in my stomach had been removed and I had healed well. I still had the fevers, but they were not as high as the previous nights.

The next day the welfare insurance kicked my baby out of the hospital. They said he was too well to be there. I, however, needed to stay because the medical staff felt I was not well enough to go home. I told them, "If my baby goes, then I go with him." They argued, saying the baby was well and I needed more tests. But I was adamant about going home with my son. I did not want to spend another day in the hospital. They made me feel worse than I was. I told them if they wanted to see me they would have to come to my house. They quickly made arrangements to do just that.

They took blood from me at a few home visits and measured the baby to make sure he was growing well. Surprisingly, I did not have a fever that night at my house or any night after that. I guess God just wanted to slow me down to show me *Himself.* It was not enough just to bring me out of the delivery alive; he wanted to talk to me about his plans and why he had done things the way he had. If you do not give God any attention, he will make sure he gets your attention.

He is a jealous God, and he does not want any other gods before him: no man, child, car, job, T.V., DVD, Internet, money, hair, drugs, nails or *church*! (Did I write that?) Yes, some of us can get so tied up "churching" that we forget to praise God. We forget that the whole reason we are in church is to learn more about God, to worship God collectively and strengthen each other as saints. Church is not a sporting activity, like we sometimes treat it. It is a place where we go

When Between Pillars - Push!

to rejuvenate our spirits from all the fiery darts that come at us in the world on a daily basis. Never let the church itself become a god. There is only One God, One Faith and One Baptism.

CHAPTER ELEVEN

Happy In Jesus Christ

If my people, which are called by my name, shall humble themselves,
and pray, and seek my face, and turn from their wicked ways; then will I hear from heaven, and will forgive their sin, and will heal their land.
                                                       2 Chronicles 7:14

After the hospital episode, I gave my life to Christ seriously! And after my son turned four weeks old, I started going to church regularly. I decided to attend the church my mother was attending where the word being preached was strong and uncompromised. After a few Sundays I decided to join. I do not know what I would have done without that church. Just watching the women of the church was enough to show me that being saved does not mean you cannot have fun. We had little get-togethers, and small seminars about how a single woman needed to act to be in line with the word of God. (This church is now my "womb church" because it helped develop me into the Christian I am today.) I was there every time the doors opened. I had become a Jesus freak. I figured any God who could deliver me from demons, death and everything in between, was someone I needed to know on a personal and regular basis.

Everyone was so into the Lord and many members had received the Holy Ghost. This was different than what I was accustomed to seeing. At the churches I had gone to in the past, if any person tried to get their praise on, every usher on the board was restraining them. I have actually been in churches in which the Spirit never hit in a way anyone knew of. No one *cried*, no one was *convicted* and no one *shouted*. I suppose they figured they were not supposed to openly show those feelings. At my mother's church they would just let loose and dance or run or scream (all decent and in order) and they did not care who was looking. I wanted the Holy Ghost so bad. I wanted to be that close to God. I wanted to feel his presence like they had. But God did not work with me like he worked with others. I had to be almost drowned in the Word and become halfway proficient with the Bible before God allowed me to receive the Holy Ghost.

God knew I was an emotional person. He did not want me in this race for the sheer emotions, because emotions will change on you and then what will you do? Go back to sin? My emotions had put me into the state of sin in which I had lived for so long. He wanted to make sure that when I hooked up with him I was in it until the end. That is not to say I did not have any problems at home. There were plenty at home because I was struggling with living with my boyfriend in sin. I did not want to leave him. I wanted to get married so I could have him and God at the same time.

When I had our son blessed, my boyfriend came to church and stood up as family with us. But we were so young and he did not seem to be ready for what I wanted. That in itself was a sign we were unequally yoked. Our incompatibility did not become evident until Thanksgiving of 1999.

I had been so excited because it was our first Thanksgiving as a family. I cooked turkey, greens, candied yams and dressing...you know how we do it on Thanksgiving. On top of that, my father, whom I hadn't seen in years, was coming in from another state to see his first grandson. I had so much to be thankful for besides life itself and being saved.

When I first got home from the hospital the old life I was used to started to creep back in, only this time I had a child to think about. Let me remind you that many times, even when we accept Jesus as our Savior, we need to understand that Newton's laws of physics still apply. Whatever you set in motion before your salvation will usually be waiting for you after your salvation. Before I was saved, I had set in motion a lot of bad and indifferent things. They were waiting for me.

We were keeping the house somewhat drug-free, but the guys would sit on our back porch and drink a beer or two. One day when the guys were out drinking on the porch the task force hit. They came in swarms of black suburbans and unmarked police cars. It turned out they had been watching the area for some time and a lot of drug trafficking went on around where I lived, but it was not me. I did not even drink anymore. It was the people in the house next door, but it was because the homes were attached and the guys hung outside *my* porch that the task force came in on us.

They legally could not have come into my house, but one of the guys came in through the back door when the cops were in pursuit and threw some weed in our dryer. The police froze the whole house and barricaded the exits in search of drugs. They tore open cabinets, arrested several of the guys who were outside, and threatened to bring the dogs in if I did not tell where the drugs were. I honestly did not know what they were talking about. When one of the officers pulled about a half an ounce of weed from the dryer, they tried to arrest me and were questioning several witnesses and asking for someone in the neighborhood to take my baby. No one volunteered, and they were forced to leave me at my house because I had not done anything illegal. They forced me to sign papers and other things and tagged my house as a dope house.

Then they gave me a weed ticket and a court notice. When you live in low-income housing, the lease says that if anyone gets arrested for anything having to do with drugs, smoking, buying, harboring or selling, you will automatically be kicked out. The police department had an agreement set up that any drug busts done on the low-income housing premises would automatically be reported to the rental office. Within a week the drug offender would be evicted. What was I going to do with a new baby and only a week left before they threw me out? I was innocent, and I explained the whole situation to the rental department. Fortunately, the lady I spoke to was the same one I ran to when I accepted Jesus. She agreed to let me stay until I went to court. But if I lost the case, I would lose my home, my child and my freedom. I would be arrested for at least six months. They wanted to pin all the drug activity in the lot where I lived on me.

Dear Lord, I know I didn't do anything and so do you. Make it so that they know it, too. I don't want to lose my baby. In Jesus' name. Amen. I showed up at court with the person to whom the weed belonged so he could tell the whole truth. No one had money for a lawyer, and I had a feeling that a public defender would just want to cut a deal. I was not cutting any deals with anyone. I was not about to lose my baby for something I did not do. Uriah was my only son and I went through too much to have him taken and to have me go to jail or to prison.

The judge let the arresting officer speak first. He had diagrams of my home and specimens and all kinds of Perry Mason/Judge Judy type things. The devil was quick to tell me I would not win this case. *If God be for me, who can be against me*, I thought. The judge let me cross examine the arresting officer and God put the words in my mouth to create reasonable doubt. When it was time for our closing comments, the officer had a lot to say. In my closing statement, I walked right up to the bench clutching my son in my arms, looked straight in his eyes and said, "I didn't do it." No fancy words; I did not even call my witness. I just said what God told me to say and *Hallelujah!* I beat the case!

So, like I said, when Thanksgiving arrived, I had a lot to be thankful for, and when my father arrived, he had a lot of family to see. My father stayed long enough to take pictures of Uriah, fix a couple of plates and pray with us before he headed back to his home. He prayed that my boyfriend and I would be a family if it were in God's will, and that everything would work out. He put his blessings on us in Jesus' name and left.

By the end of December, God decided my boyfriend and I needed to split up. Our relationship had been deteriorating and it was not pleasing in God's sight. We broke up bitterly, like some crazy skit in a soap opera, with me throwing all of his belongings out of the upstairs window and all over the lawn. I immediately gave my notice to move and within weeks I had moved into my father's and stepmother's home, which is in another state.

Moving in with my parents has been a very humbling experience. It seems as though God is trying to take me back to my teenage years and start over again, only this time I have a child. The hardest parts have been submitting myself to authority. I was on my own for so long, and called my own shots, but I cannot do that in *their* house (especially if I want God to continue blessing me enough to let me leave). What I have learned since I have lived with them are lessons for which I can never repay the Lord.

I had never seen what a married couple is supposed to be like until I moved in with my parents. I had all these ideas of what a man was supposed to be and how a relationship was supposed to go based on what I had seen on television, videos and things in school. Had I known then what I know now, a lot of drama in my life would have never happened. I see how a husband and wife are supposed to go to church together and stand unified. I had become used to seeing women in church and only a few men. I had never seen a man interact with his family when I was at an age old enough to comprehend what was going on. Just by God placing me in their midst I know what I desire in a husband, should God send one to me. I can desire the things I see in my parents' house because I know they line up with the Word of God.

My new church home is a deliverance church also. I guess God's trying to tell me something. My new church has a strong pastor who is a woman of God, and I am surrounded by real Christian women who can give me godly guidance and counseling. That is important, because even though you can get advice from your best friend, it may not line up with the Word of God, and you could end up asking someone else for advice after you have made the mistake.

Look at how God blesses when you step back and let him move. I am not saying everything is perfect. But everything is a lot better than before and I have a closer relationship with God *now* than I have had in my entire life.

I only wish I had not been so unruly when I had to go through all those health problems as a child, because God does not forget the tests he gives us. If we fail them, we have to take them again until we learn it God's way. Had I passed my test the first time, only God knows what could have been. Instead, I kept postponing the testing date, but that only made the test harder to take. I have learned that the test is unavoidable. It is like when you are in school and you pretend you are sick because of a test. When you go the next day, thinking everything is cool, you end up having a quiz. When the Word talks about studying to show yourself approved, it is not just talking about memorizing Bible verses. It means to study the Word until it gets into your spirit so that when the test comes you will have sustenance and can pass the first time. Take it from me: the re-test is *always* harder than the first test.

"Without the test, there couldn't be a testimony."
Pastor V.C. Scott

ABOUT THE AUTHOR

Singer, Songwriter and Teacher of the Gospel, Meka A. Parrish has taken pieces of her own life and candidly writes about her own deliverance through Jesus Christ. She is a mother, and a true believer in Jesus Christ. She also is an actual member and drummer at New Testament Deliverance Church in Washington, DC. No stranger to public speaking, she is a former winner of the Hawkins Award of public speaking and a former winner in The International Model and Talent Association. She also is very down to earth and honest in her writings. Finally, a writing from an everyday person.

Printed in the United States
47386LVS00005B/91-105